SHORT
COURSE IN
RUM

SHORT COURSE IN RUM

A Guide to Tasting and Talking About Rum

LYNN HOFFMAN

Skyhorse Publishing

Skyhorse Publishing books may be purchased in bulk at special discounts for sales promotion, corporate gifts, fund-raising, or educational purposes. Special editions can also be created to specifications. For details, contact the Special Sales Department, Skyhorse Publishing, 307 West 36th Street, 11th Floor, New York, NY 10018 or info@skyhorsepublishing.com.

Skyhorse® and Skyhorse Publishing® are registered trademarks of Skyhorse Publishing, Inc.®, a Delaware corporation.

Visit our website at www.skyhorsepublishing.com.

10 9 8 7 6 5 4 3 2 1

Library of Congress Cataloging-in-Publication Data is available on file.

Cover design by Brian Peterson

Photo of light molasses on page 195 by Wikipedia user Londonista

Print ISBN: 978-1-62914-727-7
Ebook ISBN: 978-1-63220-125-6

Printed in China

Contents

Chapter 1: **A Purist and a Modernist Walk into a Bar**   1

Chapter 2: **Working in the Rum Factory**   19

Chapter 3: **Why Rum Matters**   45

Chapter 4: **The Taste of Rum**   71

Chapter 5: **What Does Drinking Mean?**   97

Chapter 6: **Rum Recipes**   127

Chapter 7: **Rum and the New Alchemy**   151

Chapter 8: **Further Rum Reading (and Travel)**   179

Chapter 9: **The Short Course in Rum Tasting (SCIRT) Kit**   193

About the Author   203

CHAPTER 1

A PURIST AND A MODERNIST WALK INTO A BAR

When I started working on this book, I was pretty sure what I wanted to do. I wanted to look at noble, fragrant, complex, wood-aged rums: the type of liquor that's served in snifters and consumed slowly, even reverently. I had the suspicion—maybe even the conviction—that rum was a serious, big deal sort of thing, somewhere above single malt scotch and maybe (just) below cognac. The suspicion was fed by tastes of great, budget-priced rums (Mount Gay) and exquisite and exquisitely-expensive ones (Zacapa).

I was infused with missionary zeal. I think I was hoping to find the rum snobs of the world and go off in a corner where we could all talk about esoteric little bottlings and feel quite content with ourselves. I was a purist and I wanted to meet other purists and convert the uninitiated.

My own drinking history (see chapter 5) has only lately been touched by purism. I was never a wine snob: I was just as happy with a grapey-ripe fruit bomb as I was with an elegant super-Tuscan. I'd love a d'Yquem one day and then trot off happily with a Banyuls the next.

Beer was different. There was a lot of product out there that didn't taste very good. Some of it was so bad that the only thing it could be compared to was nauseating, sweet cocktail confections made with cheap rum. I was a beer snob almost from my first bottle of Saison Dupont.

Purism is a kind of ingredient-specific thinking. The best *X* must be the most reverently produced, additive-free example of its kind—an original recipe that outdoes others only in its adherence to some antique ideal. The real beef lover will only

The thing itself: sugarcane.

allow some salt and perhaps a crank of pepper. A true baseball fan despises the designated hitter. A proper rum enthusiast will allow nothing but sugarcane in the bottle and maybe a splash of water in the glass. And so on.

When I started some serious tasting, what I discovered made me abandon the purist approach. It even led me to question and finally reject the whole notion of purism. What derailed my approach to purism was a sudden appreciation of Modernist cooking. This epiphany happened at a tavern in Philadelphia called Kraftwork, and I'll tell you more about it in minute, but first let's talk about the Purist and the Modernist.

The Purist

You know this guy: he drinks single malt scotch, maybe the occasional cognac. He takes his liquor straight at cellar temperature in a thin-walled glass—a tumbler for the scotch, a snifter for the brandy.

He (it's usually a man) is horrified at the thought of soda, visibly pained at the notion of a cocktail.

He is a connoisseur—someone proud of his knowledge of the difference between good and bad. He's also a purist—someone who revels in, even worships the idea of a pure, uncompromised thing in itself.

He likes the solos at the jazz club, the consommés at the restaurant. He also takes a certain pleasure in the elevation of his purism above your trashy compromise. He almost needs to snort at your Brandy Alexander in order to fully enjoy his VSOP.

He's an easy object of fun, both because of the supercilious attitude that often accompanies his pronouncements and for the shaky intellectual ground on which they stand. (Was the scotch purer the minute it came out of the still? What about the adulteration of it by aging then diluting?)

But there is something sweet, almost romantic about the purist—some quality that we have to admire and to which many of us aspire. Admiring things in their simplicity, he turns our attention to the beauty in less, encourages a restrained horror of more. There is an elegance in the drink from the artisan's still or the winegrower's vat or the brewer's barrel. There is also a suitable humility in our recognition of that elegance by simply leaving it the hell alone as we put it in a glass.

The first part of our ratings is devoted to rums for the purist. These are mostly wood-aged rums that have spent five or more years thinking about themselves before they came to a liquor store near you. They are the products of sugar-cane, wood, time,

Beef Wellington.

and skill. The best thing about having a purist category is that these rums give us a chance to see what the cane has in it.

The Modernist

Suppose you could take a bacon, lettuce, and tomato sandwich on a brioche and extract all its flavors and textures and rearrange them. Imagine further that you transformed smoky bacon into a chewy roll and made crispy strips of tomato and layered them

Looks odd; tastes great.

with leaves of brioche and doughy, eggy, buttery slabs of lettuce. Does that sound awful? Does it offend the purist in you? Hmm.

The modernist position on food is that no food owns its own properties and that any manipulation we can do in service of foodie fun is not only justified, it's holy, worthy, artistic work. The aim is to create a new experience, not to honor old ingredients. So let's compress a slab of cucumber in a vacuum bag and turn it into pemmican. Then, let's sprinkle it with gin and serve it before dinner where the cocktails used to be. You're not defiling the cucumber; you're helping it realize its potential.

Once you make the sensation the center of culinary effort, you change the whole view of ingredients. Can you imagine a single-malt sorbet? Could you imagine its taste as it melts on a jelly-soft square of sous vide cooked salmon that's waiting for it in a nest of deep fried dill leaves?

One of the loveliest things about rum is that it seems to invite collaboration. It wants to drench pound cake and pull the flavor out of fruit or freeze itself with raisins into ice cream. Rum is pretty fond of other liquids too. It adds dimensions to other alcohols and elevates a host of poor, sad, non-alcoholic drinks. (Can't you hear pineapple juice over in the corner crying for its beloved rum? Imagine: without cocktail rum, a piña colada would just be smushed pineapple and coconut flavor. A rum and Coke would be . . . well, you get the idea.)

Rum's native flavors—cane, caramel, vanilla, nutmeg, allspice, dried fruit—suggest one level of collaboration and quite a few distillers have taken up the challenge and have made spiced rums. These are amplified rums with a bit of compatible outside spice added to the native cane and wood combination.

Harvesting sugar cane in the late nineteenth century, Queensland, Australia.

On another level, there are simple cane bombs that are made to whisper their way into cocktails to provide either an extra flavor or just the alcoholic raison d'être of an interesting mixed drink. We'll review those along the dimension of impact from low to high.

Modernism in cooking probably begins in France in the early 1970s with cuisine minceur or nouvelle cuisine. Cuisine minceur, with its tiny portions and elaborate plating, was easy to make fun of at first, but today its revolutionary principles seem almost axiomatic. The Gault Millau restaurant guide of 1972 listed a few of cuisine minceur's principles:

- "Culinary rules . . . must be understood but they should not be allowed to hinder the development of creative new dishes."

- "Creatively breaking culinary rules . . . is a powerful way to engage diners. . . ."
- "Diners have expectations. . . . Surprising them with food that defies their expectations is another way to engage them. . . . This includes putting familiar food in unfamiliar forms."
- "First-rate ingredients are the foundation on which cuisine is built."

The second part of our ratings is devoted to the Modernist interest in rum as a tool; as a way to evoke delight in the company of other ingredients. This kind of consideration leads naturally to the third set of ratings—a consideration of cocktails.

Cocktails

You can probably imagine how pleased I was when I saw the difference between the modernist and the purist as the key to understanding how to approach the disorderly subject of rum. Nothing like a nice dichotomy to tidy things up. In this corner, ladies and gentlemen, the aging world champion, The Holy Ingredient. In the opposite corner, the scrappy inventive challenger, Sensation By Any Means.

Unfortunately, a few minutes after I started congratulating myself on solving this book's big conceptual problem, I knew that I was at least partially wrong. The modernist depends on the quality of her ingredients, the purist (mostly) values the objects of his desire for their ability to create sensations. The Aristotelian *A*-or-not-*A* becomes the Buddhist *A*-and-not-*A*.

Zacapa in a snifter and a Dogfish Head Wit Rum Mojito are closer than you might think. I wonder if seeing them as organically connected, as each simultaneously themselves and the other, will make rum more fun to drink. We'll see.

RUM. A species of brandy . . . distilled from sugarcanes. Rum . . . differs from simple sugar spirit in that it contains more of the natural flavour or essential oil of the sugarcane . . . the flavour of rum is really the effect of the natural flavour of the cane.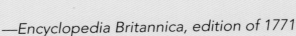
—*Encyclopedia Britannica, edition of 1771*

You may be shocked to hear that when you stop at your local liquor store, the rum section won't be divided into two sections: Purist and Modernist. The retailers have a system of their own and its categories are loosely defined.

White Rum

If you take any alcoholic drink and distill it very thoroughly, you end up with pure alcohol. Pure alcohol (I mean really pure) doesn't care about the kind of sugar from whence it came. Highly distilled alcohols all taste the same. So vodka, distilled from grain or potato, and white rum, distilled from cane juice, are going to taste pretty much alike. They will be hot on the palate with a faint sense of sweetness. They will add their aggressive character to mixed drinks but will do so without contributing much flavor of their own.

White rum is essentially a modern invention. The original distilling apparatus—alembics and pot stills—carried a lot of the flavor of the original liquid over into the distillate. It required the development of a continuous or column still in the beginning of the nineteenth century and the widespread use of charcoal filtering to strip rum of both its flavor and color.

White rums run a gamut from highly-distilled neutral spirits to lightly mineraled and earthy spirits that have a pale but definite personality. Since most white rums are used in cocktails, their lack of character makes the differences between them mostly unimportant. However, there are a few white rums that retain enough connection to the cane that they could be sipped alone or diluted with a splash of water.

Rhum Agricole

This is rum made from freshly pressed sugarcane juice instead of molasses. The use of cane juice is associated with the French West Indies but now cane juice rums are made throughout the Caribbean. The use of cane juice originated when Napoleon Bonaparte, having subsidized the beet sugar industry, prohibited the importation of cane sugar from the islands. The sugar refineries couldn't survive without exporting sugar to the mother country and so they turned to fermenting and distilling cane juice. Although the shift was in many ways an accident of history, it's hard not to notice that this method of rum production bears a resemblance to the processing of wine into Cognac and Armagnac, two beverages whose market had been earlier undercut by rum.

Rhum agricole is now produced in Trinidad, Panama, the Dominican Republic, French-speaking Haiti, as well as in Martinique, Grenada, Guadeloupe, Marie-Galante, and St. Barths. Two islands in the Indian Ocean—Reunion Island and Mauritius—also produce cane juice rum.

Cane juice rums from Martinique are labeled *AOC Rhum Agricole Martinique* in a manner reminiscent of French wine labeling laws. Martinique's cane juice rums are usually distilled to 70 percent alcohol and then diluted down to 40–55 percent for bottling. It may be aged as little as three months or for as long as several years. After three years in oak it can be marketed as Old Rum.

Fourteen distilleries produce rhum agricole. The most renowned include Clément Estate in Le Francois, Depaz Distillery in Saint-Pierre, and Saint James Distillery and Museum in Sainte-Marie. The most widely distributed cane juice rums are the Barbancourt rums of Haiti. They are aged in oak barrels for four, eight, and fifteen years.

These rums are necessarily more expensive than molasses-based rum as they don't have the sale of sugar to offset the cost of the raw material and it takes more energy to distill the lightly alcoholic liquid made from cane.

The charm of rhum agricole lies in its herbal quality: there is touch of vegetal earthiness that recalls woods and wine.

Cachaça

This is a sugarcane rum and technically speaking it's no different from rhum agricole. In point of marketing reality, it's a whole other world. Over a billion liters of cachaça are produced in Brazil every year and almost every drop is consumed there. Simple white cachaça—the vast majority of production—is remarkably cheap and is used in a variety of mixed drinks. The more complex and aged varieties are decidedly snifter worthy. In big-city bars, look for Novo Fogo Barrel Aged. In the future, we can expect to see cachaça aged in Brazilian hardwoods.

In fact, one of these drinks, the caipirinha, propelled cachaça out of the rocket-fuel stage and into the cocktail bar. (Crushed limes, sugar, and ice can round over lots of rough edges in a spirit) The caipirinha may be less fashionable today, but cachaça may still be going uptown. In 2012, Diageo, the drinks giant, bought Ypióca, Brazil's third-largest cachaça brand, paying over $450 million for the company. Look for serious promotion of cachaça-based cocktails in bars in Europe and America.

If you like your historical parallels, it's easy to point out that a curtailed market for cane sugar is again impelling the conversion of cane juice into fermented and distilled drinks. At the same time, some of Brazil's forty thousand distilleries are promoting wood-aged versions which are converging on the quality and elegance of rhum agricole.

A Spanish company called Murex has just released a "beer" made from fermented sugarcane. The first batches are all sold out. Home brewers and craft brewers in cane rich countries are pursuing the idea. Stay tuned.

Spiced Rum

It's hard to imagine spiced scotch whisky, isn't it? Just as hard to imagine spiced Cognac. You could probably go all confectionary on bourbon without the distillery gods sending down thunderbolts, but even that's a stretch. The same thinking would lead us to laugh at the idea of spiced rum and yet spiced rum sells 8 percent of the total rum market in the UK and USA and grew by almost 10 percent in 2011, making it the fastest growing category in the spirits store. The notion of spiced rum is made possible by the fact that some of rum's natural flavor echoes the flavors found in common spices. The spices in spiced rum are mostly the "baking spices": cloves, nutmeg, cinnamon, vanilla, allspice. The resemblance of the rum to liquid cake is remarkable—all that's lacking is the addition of some sweetener and we will have arrived at the ultimate teenage fantasy: an alcoholic cupcake.

History is on the side of the spiced rum lover. One observer of Barbados rum noted that it contained "red pepper for spice, which wants little of the heat of a fire coale." (This was in 1667, when rum was commonly served at twice the strength of brandy. Can you see the beginnings of rum's bad boy reputation?)

Once you allow the idea of spiced rum, the next intriguing idea is that you can make your own (see rum tasting notes and the Short Course Imitation Rum Kit).

Flavored Rum

Flavored rum is spiced rum's first cousin. Instead of baking spices providing the flavor, these rums borrow the flavors of coconut, apple, banana, mango, pineapple, lemon, lime, and other fruits. Some flavored rums are enriched with the fruits themselves, others rely on artificial replications of the main aromatic chemicals in the fruits.

If you find yourself enjoying flavored rums, you'll be happy to know that you can make exquisite versions of them using white rum and fresh fruits. Again, consult the rum-tasting notes.

Wood-Aged Rum

Now we're in the land of the grown-ups; in the company of rums that keep company with the finest (or at least the most respected) distilled spirits in the world. Wood-aged rums typically are small-batch, pot-stilled spirits (see Distillation) that retain a lot of the quality of the original fermented liquid. They are transferred from the still to wooden barrels—typically at 140 to 160 proof.

Like any wood-aged spirit, these rums lose some harshness, acquire some flavor from the wood of the barrel, and lose some of their volume to evaporation. After aging, they are diluted with water to bring them to an appropriate drinking proof and then bottled.

These rums are more expensive than the other, more easily produced types. They also tend to be cheaper than the equally ambitious spirits like scotch, bourbon, and cognac. Here's the post-colonial lesson: rum is made in places where labor is cheaper, it relies on a raw material that's inexpensive, and is grown on land which is itself inexpensive. When you enjoy great wood-aged rum, you're taking advantage of the unequal distribution of wealth in the world. Call it the import/export business, call it tourism-in-a-glass, call it a simple recognition of great taste.

Rum for the Smell of It

Bay rum is a cologne intended primarily for men. The original version, said to be from St. Thomas in the US Virgin Islands, consisted of rum, spice oils, citrus peel and the leaves of the cilliment bush, also known as West Indian Bay.

A Word about Words

The origin of the word "rum" is obscure enough to have attracted a great deal of fakelore. A lot of silliness about the word is promoted by the desire of different nations to claim credit for the drink by virtue of the name. So, some French authorities have cited the Latin word for sugar—*saccharum*—and its last syllable as the source, but the early French word for the spirit was *guildive*, a gallicization of "kill-devil" itself a term widely used in the West Indies in the seventeenth century.

The whole quality of the etymological debate is scandalously low. Let's agree that there was a predecessor in the form of *rumbullion* which appears in 1651 in Barbados and that a century earlier, *rum* was used as an adjective in England to describe something of highest quality. There is no earlier citation of the word—it's completely absent in Shakespeare.

The French word *rhum* is a complete confection: the word migrates to the French rum-producing islands as rum, with the "h" being added later by the French Academy and on the mainland.

CHAPTER 2

WORKING IN THE RUM FACTORY

A purist vision of rum might be something like this:

Rum is a combination of:

- the essence of sugarcane
- the power of the molasses that's left over from transforming cane into sugar

Now since rum made its way out into the world in wooden casks on wooden ships, it's not unreasonable for a purist to add that rum is also:

- the spirit of the wood that carried it around the world

Not a bad little purist bundle there—a raw plant, a neglected by-product, and an earthy, renewable, reusable container transformed by craftsmen into a little flavor factory.

A modernist vision might be something like this:

Alcohol is an incredible solvent of flavorful compounds. If we can get that solvent already loaded with a cargo of flavors of its own—especially flavors from the mythic, iconic, tropical sugarcane—we can probably use that as a canvas on which to paint a million other great flavors.

As you can imagine, the purists and the modernists, while they may have great respect for each other, rarely work in the same kitchen, winery, brewery, or distillery. So going to work in a rum factory required a choice: purist or modernist/tradition or innovation. There was one more distinction to watch out for: industrial or craft distilling? I decided to go for craft.

So what is craft distilling? To find out, I went to work for a few days as the most unskilled laborer in one of the premier craft distilleries in the United States. Dogfish Head is best known as an edgy, artistic, and totally modernist brewery. Their ales rarely fit the classic style descriptions that most beer lovers use to navigate the world of beer, and for that bit of eccentricity they have come to be widely respected and loved.

Dogfish Head

You may have heard about the revolution in beer. In the last thirty-five years, thousands of new breweries have opened, all of them dedicated to the idea that beer should taste good. If you weren't around before this revolution, that idea may seem so commonplace as to be not worth stating. How else should beer taste if not good?

The story has been told elsewhere—consult my book, *Short Course in Beer*, for details—but emphatically, this was a revolution created mostly by purists. The brewers who remade our notion of beer did it by returning to traditional beer recipes and allowing the flavor of beer to reemerge.

There were a few modernists—a few quirky souls who looked at the brewing process and thought that there was a tremendous potential there to create some kick-ass, world-changing, ultra-sophisticated, beguiling, and intriguing tastes. One of the modernists was Sam Calagione, who founded Dogfish Head—a high-tech, ultra-modern brewery in Delaware—and startled the beer world with brews that contained grape juice, spices, apples, raisins, herbs, citrus peel, honey. Nothing tasted traditional and everything tasted great. You couldn't write a book about the beer revolution without mentioning Dogfish and Calagione, and I didn't.

In one of those great synchronicities, it turns out that Dogfish Head is now making rum. It's no surprise that their rum is wildly modernist. The final flavors are up for grabs: no cow is too sacred to be fermented and distilled. What's truly surprising is that the distillery is about as old-fashioned and high-touch as it's possible to get. If as a wine-lover, you enjoyed the "garagistes" or if you once swapped bootleg mix-tapes of your favorite bands, you'll get the idea.

Before I take you into the Rum Factory to get your hands dirty and your palate fatigued, maybe we should pause for a brief philosophical note.

Dualism

"In each age of the world . . . will be found some profound outlook, implicitly accepted . . . almost too obvious to need expression, and almost too general to be capable of expression. [It], like the air we breathe, is so translucent, and so pervading, and so seemingly necessary, that only by extreme effort can we become aware of it."
—*Alfred North Whitehead*

Dualism is a theory about the universe, kin to one of those profound outlooks that Whitehead is talking about in the paragraph above. Dualism holds that the world is made up of two elementary categories. Good and evil, mind and body, form and

Plato and Aristotle, dualists, from Raphael's *The School of Athens*.

matter, us and them, universal and particular are examples of dualistic categories. Even though the term itself was first used in the nineteenth century, dualistic theories date back to the ancient world.

Dualisms maintain that the two categories are mutually dependent on each other and that both are necessary in the world.* Platonism, Aristotelianism, and Christianity are schools of thought based on dualism.

A major problem faced by dualists is explaining how the two realms connect. How do the mind and body relate to each other? Does the universal give rise to the particular? The difficulty involved has led many thinkers to adopt a mechanical, monistic view of the world. Scientists, for example, may deny the existence of any realm other than the purely physical. Mental and spiritual matters are reduced to brain states which are, of course. physical. Dualism disappears in the process. The utility of this kind of thinking has done a lot to advance monism as the foundation of our day-to-day modern thinking, even if we mostly remain sentimentally dualists.

In spite of the philosophical problems, some thinkers have struggled along with dualism, proposing various connections. The most persistent dualism in the western world is one that puts Mind, Spirit, and Goodness on one side and Physical Appetite, Body, and Evil on the other.

It's hard to read any western religious literature without being reminded of this distinction.

Mortify the body, purify the soul. You can see this dualism reflected in the architecture of churches which remind the worshipper with their vaulted ceilings that God is great and she (the worshipper) is very small.

* There are two other philosophical positions concerned with the number of categories: monism and pluralism. Monism is the view that there is one elemental substance whereas pluralism maintains that there are many things which constitute the world.

Spirits are the "light," alcoholic, *spiritual* fraction of a liquid, lifted away from the gross, material fraction to which they were bound. The distiller is a liberator, a transformationalist. The moonshiner is merely separating gold from gravel, wheat from chaff.

The Wash

Returning to the industrially safe and legally-sanctioned world: Rum making at Dogfish begins in their brewpub brewery, where molasses is diluted and sanitized with very hot (160°F/71°C) water and pumped into a fermenter. The yeast that's added is called distillers' yeast—it's a muscular, turbocharged, no-nonsense sort of organism that produces a lot of alcohol in a short time and doesn't contribute much flavor of its own. Two or three days later, the result is a 10 percent alcohol molasses drink

Luscious molasses. Photo by Badagnani.

(shall we call it sugarcane beer? Molasses wine? The folks who work there call it the "wash.")

Breweries are scrupulously clean places where controlling the act of fermentation is the name of the game. The brewer

Stainless steel fermenters at Dogfish Head.

ferments his beer and that's his product. The wash is not a final product, it is an intermediate step on the road to rum and its production could be pretty casual. It's fair to say that a wash produced in a brewery is about as controlled and watched-over a wash as you could get. At Dogfish, it's fermented with the same fussiness that's applied to the beer.

The fermentation is carried out with the final flavor of the rum in mind. For strongly flavored rums in Jamaican rummeries, wild yeasts and bacteria may be introduced which convert some of the sugars to acids, esters, and fusel alcohols. "Cleaner" rums start out with single-strain yeasts and may have some cane juice added to reduce the amount of cane debris or ash. The cane juice, if it's fresh, may also contain other yeasts that add to the complexity of the flavor.

This liquid is pumped out of the brewery and upstairs into holding tanks in the small distillery that perches above the Dogfish Head's brewpub.

In the days before carefully-bred and packaged turbo-yeasts, dunder was the source of the ferment. Dunder is the yeast-rich bubbling froth from a batch of rum. It was harvested to start the fermentation of a second batch. Dunder is the traditional yeast source in Jamaican rum.

Dunder is more than just yeast. It includes the yeast nutrients in the protein derived from dead yeast cells. In the old days, excess dunder would be used as fertilizer or sold as animal feed.

Unlike the beer that gets distilled into whisky or the wine that becomes brandy, the wash from the molasses doesn't taste very good. The kindest thing I can think of to say is that it's earthy. Yeah, that's a good word: Earthy.

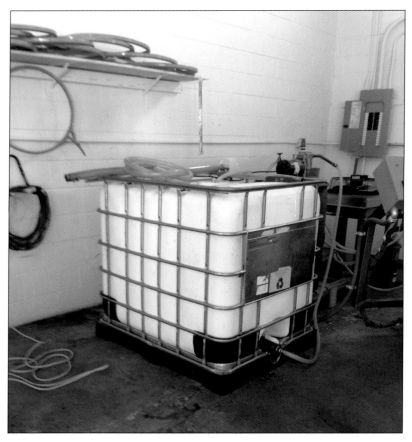

Modern container for shipping molasses.

Distilling

Work begins in the morning where 90 gallons of wash are transferred over into a stainless steel pot still. (The conical top of the still is a recycled hopper from a grain silo that was bolted onto a steam jacket and fitted with pipes and hatches. The Dogfish distillers call it the Frankenstill.)

A hand-hammered copper pot still in Austria.

The steam jacket under the still brings the temperature up and the vapors rise to the top of the pot and are led through a tube into a coil. The coil passes through a cooling water jacket (itself made from two beer kegs welded together). At first the vapor is mostly alcohol with a little water. As the distillation run progresses, the temperature rises and more water vapor makes the journey up into the cooling coil.

The vapors condense as they're cooled and they run out through a nozzle (called a parrot) that incorporates a little well. In that well, there's a measuring device—a hydrometer—which is just a float that tells how dense this condensed vapor is. Alcohol is less dense than water and so density is a good way to measure the amount of alcohol in a water/alcohol mix. Reading the hydrometer lets the distillers know when the distillation run is producing a smaller amount of alcohol.

When the alcohol yield diminishes, the heat's turned off and the remaining sludge is discarded. This first distillation is called the stripping run: most of the alcohol has been stripped out of the wash, but the product in the holding tank is a long way from being rum or even from being drinkable.

Water is one-and-a-quarter times denser than alcohol. If you throw a float in alcohol, it sinks deeper than the same float would in water. In mixtures of the two, we can tell what the proportions are just by looking at a calibrated float and seeing how high it rides. The more water in the mixture, the higher the float.

The day's work at Dogfish produces about thirty gallons of distillate at about 90 percent alcohol (180 proof). It's a pretty nasty product with traces of methanol (so-called "wood-alcohol")

A hand-made still in Sardinia, Italy.

and a harsh, petrochemical aroma. If you've ever been unfortunate enough to smell moonshine, you know what I mean.

The next day, the liquor from the stripping run is fed back into the clean still. At about 173°F, alcohol vapors begin to escape the mixture. The first vapors are called the heads and they contain most of the methanol and a lot of the harsh flavors. They're separated out and at least one of the distillers carefully tastes drops of the heads until the flavor becomes cleaner, more like molasses. Now the distillate is real rum. This heart of the distillation is collected and moved to a storage barrel. When the temperature of the vapor rises and the alcohol level in the distillate drops, the flavor changes again. The earthier end of the distillate, the tails, is also separated out.

Checking levels at Dogfish Head.

So far, so purist. What we have is a carefully curated version of fermented molasses. At some distilleries, this would go into wooden barrels; at others, it might be distilled again and filtered to remove most of the molasses flavors. At Dogfish, this

Careful tasting is the best quality control.

new rum is the heart of a new recipe. You can buy some of this pure essence of molasses, but you'll have to go to the distillery in Rehoboth, Delaware, to pick it up. Dogfish is betting on the modernists and it's not distributing this rum.

There are two small-batch rums that they are distributing, with the distillery's descriptions:

Dogfish Head Brown Honey Rum is a double-distilled amber rum made with Delaware wildflower honey and aged on American oak chips. Dark and smooth, this rum has a subtle woody character from the oak aging and a touch of sweetness from the honey.

Sounds a bit like bourbon doesn't it? Or at least something that would appeal to a purist lover of American wood-aged spirits?

The second rum is:

Dogfish Head Wit Spiced Rum. It is a triple-distilled rum aged on Curacao orange peel and coriander. This is a refreshing citrus rum that starts with a note of spiciness and ends with a citrus character.

If you've been drinking your beer like a good citizen, you'll probably recognize the orange peel and coriander as the delicious additions to white beers like Hoegaarden. What's this rum for? Well the serving suggestions include: mixed drink, soda, or Dogfish cocktail. So we have a rum that evokes the flavors of a popular beer and it's being mixed with soda . . . hmm . . . sounds like some creeping modernism to me.

New rum is sometimes treated to remove some of its character. It can be filtered through carbon granules to remove some flavor, it can be chilled and filtered to clarify it, and, of course, different batches can be blended together, coloring—in the form of caramel—introduced, and even (gasp!) flavors added.

Aging

Raw distilled spirits taste terrible. This happens because the odd products of fermentation (the congeners like acetaldehyde and the dreaded methanol) along with the volatile substances in the original fermented liquid are transferred to the distillate and concentrated by the removal of water during distillation. These harsh chemicals not only affect the taste of the spirit, they are associated with hangovers and other medical ill-effects of alcohol. They can be tamed in several ways.

Some spirits are redistilled. A second distillation that leaves the early vapors (the heads) and the last ones (the tails) behind will be higher in alcohol and lower in congeners. The three Xs you may have seen on the side of cartoon liquor jugs was a sign that the liquor inside had been distilled three times and was therefore presumed to be purer.

A more direct approach is filtration. The spirits are passed through a column of activated charcoal which absorbs the impurities. Most premium vodkas are filtered as are America's most famous sour mash whiskeys. In countries where home

Smaller barrels impart their flavor in less time.

distillation is legal or tolerated, the simple equipment for the process is easily available to hobbyists.

The most romantic—and expensive—process is barrel aging. Most premium brands of spirits that are distilled at low-proof undergo a period of barrel-aging. Putting spirits in a barrel creates some of the same changes that wood-aged wine undergoes: concentration by evaporation, addition of caramel and vanilla flavors, and oxidation of more volatile components. Bourbon and rye whiskey are required by American law to age in new, charred oak. Most spirit barrels have been previously used for wine or bourbon, so the tannic, oaky taste that you may associate with bourbon whisky or wood-aged wine has been extracted and rarely shows up in spirits.

There is no world-wide agreement about how rum should be matured, and rum is aged in many kinds of facilities and locations and for varying lengths of time. Rum can be bottled straight from the still with little or no aging or it can be aged up to thirty years in different sorts of wooden barrels. Rum can be found aging at sea level in St. Croix or thousands of feet up in the mountains in Nicaragua. In the Cayman Islands you can even find it aging underwater, presumably next to other liquid assets that are traditionally sequestered in the Caymans.

A Digression

In 1892 James Monahan, an immigrant's son in upstate New York, finished his apprenticeship as a cooper—a barrel-maker. As odd as that may seem to us, barrel-making looked like a pretty secure skilled trade for an ambitious young man.

Most things that were shipped were shipped in barrels. Barrels were the ideal container: their curved outlines made them strong enough to withstand the abuses of loading, they were watertight and relatively light compared to what they could contain, and they could be rolled and an experienced dock hand could rock one into an upright position with a few graceful pushes.

Barrel-making was a skilled craft. The skill was in short supply and the demand seemed infinite. What could go wrong?

Five years later, metal barrels were being mass-produced. They lasted longer than their wooden predecessors and cost about the same to make. Coopers preceded buggy-whip makers as the new century's first technologically unemployed.

James went on to become a cabinet-maker. His grandson eventually wrote books about wine and beer and spirits aged in—can you believe it—wooden barrels.

Bourbon Barrels?

However, one pretty constant aspect of rum aging is the widely accepted art of maturing the rum in once-used bourbon oak barrels. This is the common method of aging used by most rum producers as well as by producers of other spirits today. So why is it that rum is aged in used bourbon barrels? In 1964, the United States Congress recognized bourbon whiskey as a "distinctive product of the United States." In the resolution it

Barrel aging.

states that: "Among the standards of identity which have been established are those for 'scotch whisky' as a distinctive product of Scotland, manufactured in compliance with the laws of Great Britain, Canadian whisky is made in compliance with the laws of Canada, cognac in compliance with . . ." (by now, you get the idea)

So bourbon should be manufactured in accordance with the laws of the United States. And Congress got to work establishing those laws. One of them was that bourbon had to be aged in new, charred, white oak barrels.

As a result of this law, bourbon producers found themselves with a glut of used oak barrels and some vitality returned to the American cooperage industry. Some of these barrels had only been used for the minimum two years required by law to qualify the distilled spirit as American bourbon. Rum distillers (and other distillers and packagers) all over the world were only too glad to acquire as many of these barrels as they could get their hands on. Not only would the bourbon distillers be helping the rum distillers, it was also a way of keeping their own costs of aging their whiskey down. Today, these barrels are also used by producers of high quality beer and there's scarcely a brewer worth her hops who doesn't have at least one "bourbon-aged ale."

Whiskey extracts the most color and flavor out of the barrel in its first use. The predominant flavors extracted from the barrel are vanilla and caramel. You can't restore the new wood character to a used barrel, but you can certainly re-char it and the caramel flavor is produced mainly from the charring of the oak.

To make a barrel the American oak is cut into staves which are super-heated and bent into ovular form. The barrel is then "toasted" by sending it through a small fire for about twelve minutes to caramelize the sugar in the wood. Next, it is applied to a larger fire for six to twelve seconds to burn out the inside and produce a charcoal layer. The charring has to cover the inside of the barrel evenly so as to provide a consistent flavor to the whiskey. The larger rum producers will receive their oak barrels broken down into bundles and have their team of coopers rebuild and re-char the barrels. The smaller companies will receive their barrels in one piece and begin using them usually after a short curing process to ensure the barrels have not dried out during transport.

During the years of slow aging, the rum is said to "breathe" in the barrel. With fluctuations of temperature, the rum expands and contracts in and out of the oak barrel. This expansion and contraction of the whiskey through the caramelized layer of charred wood inside the barrel mellows it, giving it the distinctive flavor and appearance. This maturation of the whiskey happens quicker in the bourbon belt of Kentucky than it does in the cool, damp climates of Scotland and Ireland but more slowly than in the (typically) warmer climes where rum is made. A ten-year-old rum has acquired the sophistication and polish of at least a fifteen-year-old scotch. (Incidentally, this accelerated maturation is one of the reasons that beautiful rums can be had for less than comparable liquors.) The rum moves about 20 mm in and out of the one inch plus (30 mm) thick white oak, thus drawing out whatever wood flavors were left behind after bourbon aging as well as the caramel of the char.

Another result of the whiskey aging for many years in the oak barrels is that it draws many of the original flavors from the wood, but can leave behind traces of the original bourbon. In many of today's aged rums you will be able to taste slight hints of bourbon, some more than others depending on the age of the barrel it was aged in. Rum distillers may make up for the

Drum.

diminution of fresh oak (vanilla) flavor by adding wood chips or bits of discarded oak barrels into the aging rum. This provides more oak contact for the rum to draw more color and flavor.

And yes, alas, size matters. The smaller the barrel, the more contact the rum will have with the oak. The larger the barrel, the less contact with the oak. Most rum producers use a standard size barrel, around fifty-two gallons (195 liters). Others use smaller barrels for a quicker flavor transfer or huge oak vats which generally take longer to age their rums. These larger vats tend to be favored more by the French islands, for example, Barbancourt Small, artisanal rum distillers in the United States lean toward smaller barrels to hurry the process along and intensify the flavor.

All rum when it is distilled is completely colorless (no coloring agents vaporize to go up alongside the alcohol in the still). The taste is raw and penetrating. The longer the rum is aged in the barrel the darker and smoother the rum will become. Many white rums these days are aged for extended periods of time and then filtered through carbon to remove any color gained during the aging process, but leaving behind all the added flavors. For dark rums, a standardizing dose of caramel is often added to the final blend to ensure uniform color.

The Angel's Share

When rum is aged for long periods of time in an oak barrel it will slowly evaporate. This evaporation is often called the angel's share. The evaporation rate is said to be as high as 10 percent. In dry climates, water is more prone to evaporate and the aged liquor is therefore higher in alcohol. Damper aging environments encourage evaporation of alcohol and the proof is therefore lower. While the action of expansion and contraction in the oak barrel adds flavor to the rum, the concomitant evaporation is expensive and adds to the cost of aged rum: there's simply less of the product after ten years than there was at five.

Another method of aging rum that is most often employed by rum producers in Spanish speaking countries is called the solera method. Solera aging is really a process of aging and blending which muddies the question of the exact age of a rum. A solera consists of a stock of rum (or sherry or vinegar or wine) in oak barrels, divided into ranks of different maturation ages, each of equal volume. The final stage of finished rum is called the solera and the earlier ranks are the criaderas. Rum for bottling is drawn by partially draining the solera. This rum withdrawn is replaced by rum from the younger criadera, which is a little younger and less complex. Then, each criadera is refreshed with an equivalent amount of rum from its younger neighbor. The number of criadera stops before the solera varies with the distillery or winery. The result is that the rum in the bottle is a blend of rums of different ages. Some of the rum in your bottle may be as old as the solera itself.

CHAPTER 3
WHY RUM MATTERS

Let's tap the collective unconscious of the American drinking public for a moment. What do you associate with the word "rum"?

—Pirates
—West Indies
—The American Revolution
—Rum runners
—Sailors

Perhaps you have some associations of your own. Chances are that they cluster around the twin notions of bad boys and the tropics, the naughty-exotic axis. What other cultural items do we find in that psychic territory?

Rum country.

—Buccaneers

—Parrots

—Jimmy Buffet

—Tattoos

—Tricked-out hot rods

—Tiki bars

Doesn't look very serious, does it? U.S. Navy photo by Chief Mass Communication Specialist Michael W. Pendergrass.

Not very serious is it? Rum, in fact, has a place in our national psyche that marks it as both intoxicating and frivolous, an exotic cousin of vodka and something grandma splashes on pound cake. In this we are victims of our own antihistorical bias. The dizzying pace of change in the last hundred years has left us stranded. We somehow think that the way things are is the way things always have been; that the Present is the same as the Natural Order.

And yet our culture knows better. Buried in the way things are is a long chain of used-to-be's. If we get out the shovels and go below the surface a bit, we find five parallel stories that tell us why rum matters.

Part 1: Pirates

The early pirates of the Caribbean were a quasi-nation; a sort of seagoing Hell's Angels. The word "buccaneer" comes from a frame used to smoke meats. The very suggestion of a beach barbecue seems to prefigure a jug of daiquiris.

Starting around 1630, some Frenchmen who were chased from Hispaniola by the new Spanish occupation settled in the island of Tortuga. The Spaniards pursued them there but the buccaneers attracted a gaggle of Dutch and English sailors and began to use Tortuga as a base to rob Spanish shipping. Their tactics were a combination of proto-guerilla and motorcycle gang. They began by using small fore-and-aft rigged craft to attack shipping in the Windward Passage. Being lighter, their boats got more miles to the galleon. At the peak of their power, they were able to muster small armies that attacked cities on the mainland of Spanish America.

The English found the buccaneers useful. They were an inexpensive, low-risk way to wage war on Spain. Buccaneers were allowed to operate out of Port Royal, Jamaica, and they were issued letters of marque, documents that made them at least nominally more legitimate than pirates.

The Captain Morgan who, though childless, gave his name to millions of bottles of rum, was the most prominent English buccaneer and one who became famous in the English-speaking

A pirate crew and their famous appetite for rum. From *The Pirates Own Book* by Charles Ellms.

world after the publication in English of *Buccaneers of America*. He later returned to England where he was knighted.

The buccaneers quickly became a diplomatic liability; their activities in time of peace were not much different than their activities in time of war and they were suppressed and absorbed by the British in the Caribbean.

Their image, however, remains unsuppressed. For every ship that once hoisted a buccaneer ensign, there are now at least a thousand sporty young souls hoisting a buccaneer-themed rum bottle.

Part 2: American Artisans Fighting a Worldwide Mercantilistic Plutocracy

Distillation was the only industrial activity permitted in the colonies. Apples, as John Adams would be glad to tell you, were convertible to cider, and cider, of course, could be distilled and become apple jack. But it takes between sixteen and twenty-one pounds of apples to make a gallon of ordinary cider. If you distill that down to apple jack, you'd get about twelve ounces of spirit for your trouble. Transporting apples or their juice overland to the press or the distillery was expensive and the return, as you see, is low. Barley was scarce and since using it for drinks only increased the price of bread, the law often discouraged distillers from mashing grain to make spirits.

One gallon of molasses—delivered cheaply by ship—weighed no more than eight pounds. It could be diluted and ultimately converted to one gallon of rum.

The Sugar Rush

Imagine that you live in a world without *sweet*. I don't mean a world without Belgian chocolate or apple pie. I mean a world in which the taste of sweetness is so rare and expensive that you experience it only two or three times a year—perhaps in a few ripe berries or a bit of honey that is acquired at the cost of dozens of bee stings. Suppose that there aren't many other taste consolations and most of your food tastes dull. It's a world in which you are almighty grateful when the parsnips aren't too rotten and in which the weevils in the flour are a source of protein, not disgust. Imagine that there's not much variety in your food and for excitement there's a famine every few years.

Like this world so far? Good, there's more. Imagine that you hear stories from time to time about the rich tastes of faraway lands. Imagine that the few very wealthy people in your city are rumored to eat things with *flavor*.

Keep imagining. Imagine that you are a merchant with money and ships at your disposal. Imagine further that there is a whole market of these taste-starved wretches who are just getting some money to spend. Imagine that you have a product to sell them and imagine that the product is sugar.

Of course you would become stinky-rich.

If you've been imagining right along with me, you've projected yourself into Europe at the beginning of the sixteenth century. You are standing on the brink of the very first consumer-driven economic revolution.

Sugarcane was being planted in Puerto Rico, Cuba, and Hispaniola a few years after Columbus arrived. The Spanish had learned about cane when they were an Arab colony and they brought cuttings from the few small cane gardens in the homeland and the Canary Islands.

Sugar refining leaves behind it a sweet liquid called molasses. It has enough sugar to ferment itself into a weak alcoholic beverage. Distill that beverage and you have rum. It was not too long before rum became almost as important economically as the sugar itself.

Rum was introduced to Europeans shortly after the Dutch began to organize the production of brandy (*brandewijn* or "burnt wine") along the Atlantic coast of France. The first still was set up in 1624 and by 1660 the area was the center of an industry that supplied Northern Europe with its first distilled beverages. Brandy was popular for all the reasons that rum was to become so: it was compact, it didn't spoil, and it could be used to sanitize water. It preserved good wines and strengthened weak ones. Along with the intoxicating effects of wine and beer, it delivered an instant warming flush that must have been very comforting in the days before central heating.

Brandy created the market, the institutions, and the demand. Rum and the more rustic whiskey from Scotland and Ireland took advantage of lower costs: cheaper labor, and, in the case

An early still on St. Croix.

of rum, an essentially free raw material, and fuel for distillation that came from the cane plant itself.

The flood of wealth that came from sugar and rum changed the world. We still live with and cope with institutions and problems created by the trade in sugarcane products.

Part of the legacy of the trade in sugar and rum is slavery.

Sugarcane requires a lot of hand labor. The Spanish enslaved the Carib natives to work the cane, but they died in slavery. Rum proved to be cheap to make. It was also an easily transportable and attractive commodity to trade for slaves in Africa. Since distillation was an industry that the British allowed their American colonies, Yankee merchants were soon making rum and trading in slaves and sugar.

In service to sugar and rum, millions of Africans were transported to America, agricultural colonies like Massachusetts and Pennsylvania became manufacturing giants, and a handful of backward European nations became the first world powers.

Slavery was already a common household institution in Spain. The Spanish particularly prized domestic slaves from Russia and Scandinavia for their fair complexions and exotic hair color. But the need was not for slaves as ornaments, the need was for a massive infusion of labor, and that need would not be met at the gentlemen's slave markets on the Black Sea. So European merchants, first Spanish, then Portuguese established a trade with Africa. European manufactured goods were traded for African people.

The West Indies moved to the center stage of world politics. Did you ever wonder why the English, Dutch, and French fought so often for those tiny islands? The British lost more soldiers in the Caribbean than they did in Peninsular War against Napoleon. They sent more men to Haiti than they ever invested in the American War of Independence. They weren't looking for a place to vacation, they were looking for a convenient place to grow the extremely lucrative sugarcane. The value of the English trade with Jamaica was five times that of their trade with the thirteen North American Colonies. The Gold Rush may have changed California, but the Sugar Rush changed the world.

Questions of History

After rum's development in the Caribbean, the drink's popularity spread to colonial North America. The first rum distillery in North America was set up in 1664 on Staten Island (which was not then and still today may not be a part of New York City). Boston, Massachusetts, had one three years later. The manufacture of rum became early colonial New England's largest and most prosperous industry. The Mid-Atlantic and New England colonies had the technical, metalworking, and cooperage skills and abundant lumber to fuel the stills, and it was cheaper to transport molasses from the Caribbean and make the rum where the market was. North American rum was lighter, more whiskey-like. Rhode Island rum was even used, along with gold, as an accepted currency in Europe. Estimates of rum consumption in the American colonies before the American Revolution had every man, woman, or child drinking an average of 3.6 US gallons (14 liters) of rum each year. By contrast, the corresponding figure for 2013 for all distilled spirits was just under one gallon for every adult.

The disruption to the trade caused by the Sugar Act in 1764 may have even helped cause the American Revolution. In the slave trade, rum was also occasionally used as a medium of exchange. For example, the slave Venture Smith, whose history was later published, was said to have been purchased in Africa for four gallons of rum plus a piece of calico. Of course rum didn't create its own market—the taste for spirits had been cultivated on the West African coast by the Portuguese and French who competed successfully with the Arab slave traders—from Timbuktu and elsewhere—who had been there for more than two centuries.

The popularity of rum continued after the American Revolution, with George Washington insisting on a barrel of Barbados rum at his 1789 inauguration.

Rum started to play an important role in the political system; candidates attempted to influence the outcome of an election through their generosity with rum. The people would attend the hustings to see which candidate appeared more generous. The candidate was expected to drink with the people to show he was independent and truly both a Republican and a Democrat. Later, after rum was eclipsed by corn whiskey, in a Mississippi state senate election, one candidate, Judge Edward Turner, poured his drinks and socialized with the people. He was more personal and it appeared as if he was going to win. The other candidate, a Methodist parson named Dick Stewart, announced he would not be pouring their drinks and they could have as much as they wanted; Dick Stewart won.

After the American Revolution, the restrictions on rum from the British and French islands of the Caribbean embodied in the Embargo Act, combined with the development of American whiskey, led to a decline in rum's popularity. Whiskey distilled from grain took its place. Today, you can see faint echoes of the prominence of molasses in Boston baked beans and the occasional cookie.

Part 3: The Demon Rum and Slavery

"...so you see Sir, that the Juice of the Cane is made into three considerable Commodities, viz, Sugar, Treacle and Rumm."

—Thomas Tenison, 1684

One of the most puzzling aspects of researching this book was running across the calm assertion on the part of many socially conscious folk that rum was deeply involved in, indeed almost the cause of, the trade in slaves. The story is that rum, produced by slave labor in the West Indies, was carried to Africa where it was traded for kidnapped people who were then themselves sold into slavery. Rum was both the medium and the motive of one of the most odious businesses in human history.

I felt obliged to talk about this: to cite an example or two of a ship sailing from, let's say Boston or Philadelphia, laden with slave-made rum bound for the Guinea Coast of Africa. Or maybe I could find a vessel that sent rum to Europe and then proceeded to Africa laden with money to buy enslaved people. I have to admit that I had even rehearsed a few dramatic sentences to talk about the horror of it all: how the good ship so-and-so set out with a cargo of spirit and returned with a "cargo" of doomed humanity.

Of course, I never thought that rum itself was culpable—we human beings have worked too hard at being vile to have the credit snatched away by a mere commodity. But still, the story had to be told.

The only trouble was that I couldn't find much evidence of rum-for-slaves. What's more, it didn't seem that the trade in rum was big enough to account for much of the commerce in

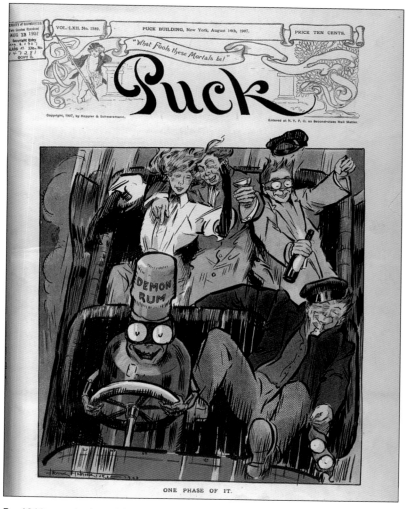

By 1919 rum had vanished from American glasses, but retained its power in the American imagination.

humans. The vast wealth of the slave-plantation economy was based on sugar: rum was an afterthought.

But somehow, everyone knows about the connection between rum and the slave trade. Where did that knowledge come from? The answer turned out to be surprisingly concrete. Rum was blamed for slavery, or at least lumped with it in a noxious fusion of immorality in the 1870s as the Temperance Movement (a most intemperate movement) sought to link itself to the victory of the United States over the Confederacy and the consequent end of slavery in America.

Before the Civil War, the enemies of drinking were hardly the enemies of slavery. Consider this speech from a prominent free black advocate of Temperance:

> "... such is the prejudice against the coloured man, such the hatred, such the contempt in which he is held, that no temperance society in the land would so far jeopardise its popularity as to invite a coloured man to stand before them. He might be a Webster in intellect, a Channing in literature, or a Howard in philanthropy, yet the bare fact of his being a man of colour, would prevent him from being welcomed on a temperance platform in the United States."
>
> —from an address by Frederick Douglass, Scotland 1846

The connection in popular sentiment between rum and slavery was cemented in the 1870s and 1880s. The Temperance advocates—we may now call them The Drys—worked the emotional connection between alcohol and slavery. It helped that in America, "rum" had become a synonym for all distilled liquors even though the consumption of rum itself declined after the Embargo Act of 1807. The "demon rum" consumed by Americans that excited proponents of Temperance and later Prohibition was almost entirely rye, corn, and bourbon whisky.

In fact, in England Abolitionists had identified the economic mainstay of slavery by the end of the eighteenth century. A merchant of Haverhill, Suffolk, advertised in the *General Evening Post* on March 6, 1792, to his customers that he would no longer be selling certain sugars. He declared:

> "... Being Impressed with a sense of the unparalleled suffering of our fellow creatures, the African slaves in the West India Islands ... with an apprehension, that while I am dealer in that article [sugar], which appears to be principal support of the slave trade, I am encouraging slavery, I take this method of informing my customer that I mean to discontinue selling the article of sugar when I have disposed of the stock I have on hand, till I can procure it through channels less contaminated, more unconnected with slavery, less polluted with human blood ..."

> —James Wright, a Quaker merchant in an advertisement, 1792

The connection between slavery and sugar is so profound and systemic that its legacy is alive today, not just in the world's sugar addiction but in the very nature of most industrial processes. Sugar production on any large scale demands intense and almost continuous labor. The growing season for cane is the entire year and the crop must be tended—planted, weeded, harvested—constantly; there is no agricultural off-season in the tropics. Once harvested, the cane is extremely fragile. Harvested cane has to be crushed within a day or its sugar content is lost. The cane juice, called guarapo, has a similarly short lifespan—a day or two at the most.

Sugar production for maximum profit was a round-the-clock enterprise. The ideal sugar mill started crushing and

Guarapo is a popular soft drink in Southeast Asia, South Asia, and Latin America. The peeled cane is run through a press. It can be served chilled and it can also have other ingredients added—lemon and lime are common in Brazil and Cuba, ginger or mint in India. In Cuban sections of Miami and Cuban-influenced bars elsewhere, cane juice is produced daily and used as a cocktail ingredient.

boiling cane at one a.m. on Monday and took a breath on Saturday at midnight. (The sanctity of the Sabbath had to be preserved.) It sounds a lot like modern factory production, but the factory was a sugar refinery first and a distillery second. The profit from sugar in the seventeenth and eighteenth centuries was so impressive that the sugar islands didn't waste valuable

Of course, before refrigerated shipping, only some food could be transported to remote tropical islands. Rice and dried corn could stand the abuse; so could salted cod fish and dried beans. Any visitor to the Caribbean today will tell you that these remain staples of the local diet.

cane fields by growing food. They were wealthy enough from sugar to import what they wanted to feed both master and slave.

One of the most exhaustive first-person accounts of Caribbean slavery is the diary of Thomas Thistlewood. From 1758 to 1786, Thistlewood lived off the labor of enslaved people in Jamaica. His kept a diary during that time which runs to fourteen thousand handwritten pages and is for most of us, very tough reading. Thistlewood's management techniques were exceptionally brutal: he is the very portrait of the evils of slavery. What is remarkable is that in these elaborately detailed accounts—there is an entry for almost every day of his life in Jamaica—there is no mention of rum. Sugar is made and sold, garden crops harvested and marketed, but no rum. Twenty-eight years of business based on the labor of slaves, lots of sugar, and no mention of rum.

Part 4: Outlaw Americans Fighting Prohibition

Rum-running. What a wonderfully jaunty phrase; it sounds more daring than illegal. *Revenuer.* What a miserable, crabbed thing, Scrooge at the cocktail party. It's no secret that Prohibition opened up another civil war in the United States. To grossly oversimplify: On one side, Prohibition as enforced by the Federal Government and the political clout of the American heartland; On the other, the Demon Rum, as personified by the urban, coast-dwelling immigrants and their children.

The original image was from the Anti-Saloon League.

Now if this were a game, I trust that we'd all be betting on Demon Rum and his squad of Rum Runners. We might even consider the resistance to Prohibition to be a bit of a triumph for rum. Here's a bit of play-by-play:

When Prohibition began in January 1920, there was a burst of smuggling activity in American ports. Coast Guard and Customs responded; waterfronts in New York and Baltimore were easy to patrol and distilled spirits in bottles were relatively bulky and easy to spot. One of the early smugglers was Captain William McCoy who began bringing rum from Bimini and the rest of the Bahamas into south Florida. His boats sailed through Government Cut, a manmade channel between South

A Brooklyn saloon on the night before Prohibition went into effect.

Miami Beach and Fisher Island, Florida. The Coast Guard soon caught up with him, so he bought a capacious Gloucester knockabout schooner and renamed it Tomoka. His new strategy was to bring his rum to just outside US territorial waters. Meeting him there were smaller boats and other captains who could make the speedy trip and unload anywhere along the coast.

Tomoka became famous and so did his cargo. Rum-running became a synonym for all the (then) illegal importation of alcohol into the country. McCoy had two other ships that hauled other alcohol: Irish and Canadian whiskey, brandy, gin, and wine. He supplied ports from Maine to Florida, but his fame and enduring reputation came from moving rum to Miami.

McCoy's smuggling career ended in 1923 after an armed battle (!) with the Coast Guardsman Seneca, but he is credited with the idea of bringing large boats just to the edge of the

A rum runner as seen from the deck of a Coast Guard cutter.

McCoy never watered or relabeled his merchandise and he concentrated on only the most-expensive, high-margin brands. The story is frequently bandied that this is the origin of the term "The real McCoy" although the phrase was used in print almost forty years earlier.

three-mile limit of US jurisdiction, and there selling his wares to "contact boats," local fishermen and small boat captains. He was also known to service float planes and flying boats. He was quickly imitated; the three-mile limit became known as "Rum Line" and the ships waiting there were called "Rum Row." The Rum Line was extended to a twelve-mile (19.3 km) limit by an act of the United States Congress on April 21, 1924, which made it harder for the smaller and less seaworthy craft to make the trip.

By far the biggest Rum Row was off the New Jersey coast, where as many as sixty ships were seen at one time. In 1923, coincident with five hundred thousand people attending the Bathers' Review—a parade—Nucky Johnson was able to boast of Atlantic City: "We have rum, wine, women, song, and slot machines. I won't deny it and I won't apologize for it."

Although rum was a minority spirit in the smuggling business, it got most of the glory.

"Rum has a definite literary advantage over whiskey. It has just three letters, one syllable and it rhymes with dumb, bum and conundrum."
—Emanuel Cardoso

premium even if the booze is not. Marketing to Millennials and Gen X is easy if you have purist values on your side. Throw in an appeal to "local" and you can sell almost anything once. But an expensive bottle of Old Local Purist that doesn't taste very good is likely to be the only one that even the most enthusiastic booster will buy.

So this industry is due for a shakeout. What can we expect in five years or ten?

First, a lot of inexpert distilleries will fall by the wayside. The investment is substantial and the production cycle long and lots of folks will be going out of business. In a year or two you should be able to search the internet for some good cheap used distillation equipment.

Second, spirits making is a skill: it can be learned. So we should expect people to start learning it. Look for distilling certificate courses at the University of California, Davis, Drexel, or the Institute for Culinary Education. We may also see Flying Distillers—skilled artisans who provide supervision to several distilleries at once. Don't you think there's a person up in the Hebrides who might want to spend his winter making rum in New Orleans or even Key West?

Finally, expect a Modernist Revolt. The definition of what to expect when you taste rum is going to change and diversify. Look for subtle spicing, remarkable smoothness, echoes of spice combinations from other drinks and foods. The name "rum" will probably be attached to most of these new developments just because of its jaunty, buccaneering, prohibition-defying, revolutionary associations. The Cocktail Revolution will continue— bartenders will indeed be the new alchemists, transforming their materials into a new sense of the sense of taste. I think it's going to be fun.

Your children may sip a sugarcane spirit that reeks of lychee nut and is flavored with the leaf of nasturtium. I'll bet that they will call it rum.

CHAPTER 4

THE TASTE OF

OF

RUM

Sugarcane yields sugar when the stalk is crushed and its juice extracted. The juice is reduced by boiling and the sugar is crystallized. The liquid left behind is the molasses. It contains about

Harvesting sugar cane, the source of rum's flavor.

5 percent sugar. Along with fermentable sugar, this molasses contains the concentrated flavor of the cane itself and the flavor of sugar caramelized during the reduction of the original juice.

Fermented molasses is, with a few exceptions, the raw material of rum. Traditionally, the molasses was fermented by wild yeasts in a slow fermentation that introduced its own complex flavors. This is still the practice for most premium rums today. The notable exceptions are the agricultural rums of the French West Indies that are made from the cane juice itself.

Most modern day rum is produced by distilling molasses in large column stills that operate continuously. These stills turn out a high proof, highly refined, and neutral tasting product. It may be as much as 190 proof (95 percent alcohol). This is the rum that gets mixed with three different kinds of fruit juices and served with a little paper umbrella on the edge of the glass. It is sometimes wood-aged, and sometimes very good. It is certainly an excellent foil for juices and sodas.

Ruins of a sugar factory, Christiansted, St. Croix, US Virgin Islands.
Photo by Jet Lowe.

A small amount of the world's total rum production is made in small inefficient pot stills like the one at Dogfish Head. These stills are loaded with a batch of fermented molasses or fermented cane juice which is then distilled at a fairly low 140-160 proof (70 to 80 percent alcohol). Pot stills are also used in the production of bourbon, single malt whiskies, and cognac. These inefficient stills leave a lot more of the original cane flavor behind. The rum from pot still production is more likely to be aged in wood (see also Working in the Rum Factory).

It is also more likely to be consumed in a snifter with only a splash of water or a few shavings of ice. It is this premium rum that is the subject of so much enthusiasm and is the ultimate subject of this book.

Questions of Value

Great Rum is relatively cheap when you compare it to spirits of similar quality. Several things conspire to make it so.

First of all, the raw material is cheaper. Molasses is a byproduct of sugar making; Serendipitous Waste you might say. By the time molasses is available for fermenting, the cane has already paid for itself in the form of sugar. It would be wrong to say that molasses is free, but compared to the grapes that make cognac or even the barley that makes scotch, it's very cheap indeed.

Some rum is made by fermenting the cane juice itself and that's even cheaper.

Rum, like other fine liquors, is aged in wood to develop complexity and smoothness. The lower cost of raw material means that less money is tied up when the product is stored for long periods of time. Fifteen years of age on a bottle of rum costs a

Making molasses is hot work. Photos by Marion Post Wolcott.

lot less than the same age on a bottle of scotch. The longer the storage period, the greater the price advantage for the rum.

Furthermore, rum tends to be aged in warmer places than other liquors. Heat accelerates the transfer and maturation of flavors in a wooden barrel, so a ten-year-old rum is more mature than a more northern spirit.

The labor is cheaper too. Most of the world's rum comes from countries that are just beginning to industrialize. Single malts and brandies come from mature European economies where workers' time is very expensive.

The price of fine aged rums also is cushioned by the availability of tremendous quantities of un-aged, almost neutral rum that's sold as a mixer. This rum is very popular. It has more flavor than vodka and consumers seem to be choosing it more every year. Most producers of fine rum do not derive their income solely from the sale of their best products to a few snifter sniffers. Instead, they are supported by a legion of rum-and-cokers, a battery of blender-wielding bartenders, and a mob of brunchers ordering rum screwdrivers and Bloody Marys.

Finally, rum doesn't have much snob appeal yet. You aren't likely to be paying much for decanters, advertising, or two page magazine spreads explaining what rum is and why you should like it.

Storage and Service

Distilled spirits age and improve in wood. Once spirits leave the barrel and enter the bottle, development stops. Those bottles of rum or cognac that you've been saving in the cellar aren't getting better, they're just getting older. That means that the rum whose label proclaims it to be twelve years old stays twelve years old no matter how long you keep it.

Once a bottle is opened, the flavor begins to deteriorate. The changes are slow, but a bottle of any spirit that's been opened for a few months will taste different than a freshly opened one. If you have a bottle of premium rum that's been open for a while, you might want to try an experiment with a new bottle of the same rum to see if the difference is noticeable or noxious.

Whatever you do, resist the temptation to pour your rum into a lead crystal decanter and store it there. I know that the decanter is a beautiful light catching sculpture and that there's something about elegant glassware that makes everything taste better. But it's also true that the sparkle and the hefty feel of your prized decanter come from the large amount of lead that

Fine, lead-free crystal shows off the beauty of wood-aged rum. Photo by Rod Waddington.

its glass contains and that this lead will slowly leach out into your rum. Lead, in case you hadn't heard, is bad for you.

You don't have to throw out your heirloom decanter; you can use it safely if you pour your rum into it just before serving and return leftover rum to its low-lead ordinary glass bottle when you're done. If you're buying someone a wedding present, it's nice to know that there are lead-free decanters coming to an expensive store near you.

A fine wood-aged rum invites you to slow down and pay attention to it as you drink. I think that the right response to that invitation is to get the most flavor and enjoyment from the smallest quantity of alcohol. Your choice of a glass can help you do that. The ideal rum glass is shaped like a tulip: a 1.5 ounce (42 ml) portion of rum should just reach the level of its widest part. The walls of the glass should taper inward from there, ending two to three inches (five to seven cm) above the level of the rum. The top of the glass should be no less than two inches (five cm) in diameter. This is shown with greater clarity in the accompanying illustration.

Maybe this glass looks familiar to you.

That's right, it's called a snifter, and it's the traditional glass of choice for cognac for all the same reasons that make it work so well for rum. Larger versions of the same glass enhance the flavor of wine and beer. The stem and base of the glass are common but optional, it could just as easily have a flat bottom[*] for greater stability.

---

[*] A company that wanted to seize the pole position in the race to market wood-aged rum might benefit from distributing a distinctive stemless snifter with molded indentations for the drinker's thumb and first two fingers.

The reason for this particular architecture is that the aroma of the rum you drink comes from its evaporated vapors. You want the greatest possible surface of your rum exposed to the air to create those vapors, so the widest section of the glass should

The perfect rum glass.

be right where the level of the rum lies. As the vapors rise, the tapering walls of the glass concentrate them. The two inch opening is large enough to accommodate the upper lip and nose of most adults of our species.

Glasses should be clean. Check them with your eye and also with your nose. Glasses should also be well rinsed. A soapy film left on a glass is as destructive of flavor as dirt or grease. An alkaline dishwashing detergent, like the kind used in automatic dishwashers, is best. Speaking of grease, don't make that exquisitely clean and neutral glass greasy with your lips. Fats from foods contaminate glasses and ruin flavors. If you've just gorged on potato chips, wipe your lips before you taste. If you're wearing lipstick, do the same.

Is there a proper serving temperature for rum? You bet there is. The problem is figuring out just what that temperature is. As a liquor gets warmer, it gives off more vapor, and the more vapor, the more flavor. Before you install a snifter warmer in your bar, remember that at very warm temperatures the predominant flavor is going to be that of alcohol. You don't want to feel the blast of pure alcohol when you drink, you want the subtle flavor that the rum picked up in all those years of aging.

As a liquor gets colder, it becomes thicker. Vodkas and white rums that are served at about 32°F have a sensuous, oily quality. They also seem less alcoholic. This can be a pleasant curiosity of a sensation with a neutral spirit like vodka or a simple one like the caraway-flavored akvavit. Frozen aged rum, however, is a waste. There's a small echo of the original flavor as the tiny residue in your mouth warms up and a mild burning sensation in your esophagus. It's not what I paid my money for.

My own tests suggest that the best temperature for serious, barrel-aged rum is just a little below what we like to call "room" temperature. Sixty to sixty-five degrees might be right. This makes for a refreshing cool sensation in your mouth and allows the rum to release its flavor as it warms. If you don't have a cellar or a cool window sill, chilling your glass will cool the rum slightly. So will a splash of cold water or an ice cube. Again, it's a question that's worth an experiment.

Water and Ice

The addition of water to your rum isn't sacrilegious. When the rum was distilled and aged it was at a much higher proof than you would want to drink (try a drop of 151 proof rum on your tongue for a moment to get the idea). So water is added before the rum goes into the bottle. The makers of the rum have already diluted it for you, so you can feel free to further dilute it to your taste. Typically, fine rums are distilled and aged at about 160 proof or 80 percent alcohol. The rum in the bottle is rarely above 90 proof or 45 percent. On some rum producing islands, the rum is delivered to taverns in casks at very high proof. When you order, you are given a shot of rum in a tall glass and a pitcher of water, so rum and water is very much in the tradition. Even if you are on one of the fortunate islands and the water in question is solid ice, it's still all right and proper. Of course, you will want the water itself to be pure and refreshing.

Taste

Do you remember being a kid and having to take an unpleasant medicine? You probably had a few techniques to shut out the taste like holding your nose and gulping the stuff down as quickly as you could. Your parents may have chilled the medicine to make its vile aromas less volatile and therefore less likely to fly up to your nose. They may have even followed the dose with a sweet drink or a cookie. Maybe you learned to distract yourself so your attention wouldn't have to be on the horrible taste and, of course, you sped through the process to get it over with.

The strategy for rum tasting is the precise opposite. You approach the process slowly, focus your attention on the aromas, linger over the flavor. You will look for food that complements the flavor. You will hold the rum in your mouth for a few extra seconds, you linger—even luxuriate.

Your goal is to extract the greatest experience of flavor from the rum, so don't be in a rush to decide whether you "like" a particular rum or not. Suspend judgment for as long as you can. The minute you decide that you "like" the rum (or not) you stop noticing the rum and start paying attention to your judgment. Your evaluation gets in the way of your perception and tasting is a game of sharpening perception.

Tasting is a lot more fun if you eliminate distractions and concentrate on the rum. You might want to banish competing aromas: no perfumes, colognes, or fruity shampoos in the air. It's also a good idea to turn the volume down on other stimuli as well. Imagine an afternoon in the shade on a deserted beach. Don't talk if you don't have to and keep other sounds down to a minimum.

See

Look at the rum in your glass. Are there sheets of liquid forming a few inches up the side of the glass and falling gently back down to the surface of the rum? Those are called **legs** or **tears**. They occur because the alcohol evaporates from the surface of the rum and the remaining water molecules, by virtue of a mutual attraction called surface tension, rise up to escape the alcohol solution below. If the side of the glass is clean, the water molecules—in search of their own company—climb up the side until gravity overtakes them and they cascade back down. It's a pleasant little sight, but it means nothing about the rum except that it has alcohol and is in a clean glass.

Be sure to notice the color of the rum too. Hold your glass up to the light and inspect the thin line of liquid where the rum meets the side of the glass. Rum fresh from the still is necessarily clear: the vapors that rise from the kettle can carry aroma and flavor but not color. Rum gets its color from being aged in a barrel or from the deliberate addition of caramel. As with beer, color in rum is a liar, but it's often used suggestively: clear rums evoke the purity of vodka or the raw power of moonshine; dark rums suggest complexity, spiciness, or fruitiness.

With the glass held against a white background, try to probe the deepest color the rum has to offer. This is a moment for poetry. What do you see? Walnut? Mahogany? Cedar? One of the best things about attending to the color is that it slows you down and adds the spice of anticipation to your cup. Some thoughtful rum drinkers have extended this attitude to other areas of their lives and swear they have profited from it.

Swirl and Dilute

Swirl the rum in the glass to increase evaporation and release the bouquet.

Your sense of smell is, after all, excited only by airborne molecules that escape from the rum. It just takes a few escapees to do the job (some aromas can be detected at concentrations of as little as one part per trillion). When you swirl, you coat the inside of the glass with a layer of rum and that layer releases aroma into the air as much as the rum in the bottom of the glass.

If the rum is over-chilled, holding the bowl of the glass in your hand or pouring it carefully into another glass can help make the aroma more available.

This is also the time to add a bit of water. Water dilutes aroma and flavor of course, but it also tames the sensation of raw alcohol and lets other flavors emerge. Alcohol has a taste of its

There's an odd bit of arithmetic in the chemistry of that splash of water in your rum. If you mix 2 ounces of water into 2 ounces of 190 proof rum you don't get 4 ounces of diluted rum, you get about 3.9 ounces. The repudiation of common-sense arithmetic has to do with the different sizes of water and ethanol molecules. Water molecules are bigger so the smaller ethanol fits in the spaces between the water molecules. It's a little like that old story about the gallon bucket filled with rocks into which you can still pour a half-gallon of sand. You can add the sand to the "full" bucket because the sand goes in the spaces between the rocks.

Incidentally, you can pour a cup or two of rum into the sand-rock mixture. This proves, I'm told, that no matter what, there's always room for rum.

own, a bit sweet with a hint of bitterness, but it can also impart a painful, mouth-burning sensation. You may find that adding water to your glass makes the rum taste harsh for a minute or two.

Sniff

Your sense of smell is a faculty located on two small patches of tissue called the **olfactory epithelium**, which is located inside your skull behind your nose and at the same level as your eyes. Your smell patch contains some five million receptor cells—

The sense of smell conceptualized as something primitive and erotic. Mural in Library of Congress Jefferson Building by Robert Reid.

about the same number as can be claimed by a mouse. In normal breathing, only 5 to 10 percent of inhaled air reaches this sensory receptor. You can increase the amount of stimulation at the epithelium by a factor of ten simply by using your nose to take sharp, deep sniffs before you drink. Loud nasal honkings that would be inappropriate at the dinner table are in order at a rum tasting. You'll notice that if you sniff a second time, your impression is diminished, a third attempt and you notice even less—the nose fatigues quickly. Don't decide if you like the aromas: just try to notice and name them.

If you notice aromas—the proper rum word is **bouquet**—but can't find the names for them, look at the Short Course in Rum Tasting checklist at the end of this chapter for some hints.

Synesthesia

This is also the time to notice that we humans easily confuse smells with tastes. This is one form of synesthesia, the mushing together or confusion of two separate senses. The evidence suggests that most people are prone to merging taste and smell: in fact, *sweet* is one of the most common adjectives applied to odors. In one study, 139 people were asked to describe a chemical used as banana flavoring in pastries. Seventy-six of the subjects volunteered that the aroma was sweet, only sixty said it was banana-like and seventy-three reported it was fruit-like. Tests of strawberry and caramel aromas gave similar results.

The folks who study this sort of thing are inclined to think that we learn these associations from them being usually paired—caramel aroma goes with sweet taste, etc. What's interesting for the rum taster is the fact that deliberately taking this particular hallucination apart leads us to greater awareness of both taste and smell.

So: does the rum smell sweet? Not really, but what aromas remind us of sweetness?

Sip

Swish the rum around in your mouth to get the maximum contact between it and your tongue and also to increase your sense of the bouquet. Keep the rum moving: **taste buds** get fatigued too. You may enjoy noticing that different sensations are detected in different parts of your mouth and tongue. Remember to notice as much as you can without deciding if you "like" the rum or not.

This is the time to notice how the rum feels in your mouth. Notice how thick or thin the rum seems to feel. This sensation is called **body**. Thin-bodied rums feel like water or skim milk in the mouth; big bodied rums are more like cream. Rum can also feel smooth or harsh in the mouth. At one extreme is the "hot" punishing experience of rum that's fresh from the still. At the other is the smooth and rich taste of barrel-aged rum (see the section on barrel aging in chapter 2).

With your mouth full, part your lips a little and draw some air over the rum. Gurgling sounds are permitted. You'll smell it a second time as the air brings the bouquet around to your "back smell."

What's happening here is that airborne molecules reach your olfactory patch through passages in the nose, but they also get there through the mouth and rear nasal passages. Since it is stimulated with the rum in the mouth, the "back smell" can be more powerful and evocative and more like a true experience of flavor.

Swallow or Spit

There's a part of the sensation of rum that you can only experience by swallowing, but sometimes there's more rum to be tasted than can be comfortably or sanely drunk. At any tasting where there are more than four or five rums, you will find spittoons or spit cups.

Discreet spitting is a rum taster's skill, which in itself is worth a little practice. You really don't want to blow a spray of Mount Gay on yourself or your fellow taster. Pull your cheeks in like a trumpet player, curl your tongue into a groove, and blow the rum out under light pressure.

Pay attention to the aftertaste, or **finish**. Does it seem like a natural extension of the flavor? How does it feel? Does the flavor last as long as the feeling of heat in the mouth?

Putting It All Together

Tasting isn't just a matter of taking a rum apart and trying to see how many separate taste points you can discover. You pay attention to individual tastes because all together, they make up the impression of the rum. The situation is not unlike that of the careful listener at an orchestral concert. Attending to separate instruments, the concert-goer nonetheless is experiencing the total harmony of all the sounds, and that, after all, is what the composer had in mind.

So at the end, after the last taste has reverberated its way off your tongue, you're going to try to grasp the big picture, to "understand" the rum. It may be helpful to think of rum's harmony in three dimensions:

- Begin with the structure of the rum: its sweetness, astringency, alcohol, acidity, and texture in the mouth. This is an easy place to start because these characteristics are easy to notice.

  Taken all together, the elements of structure in a harmonious rum can make a small, subtle impression or a big, powerful one.

- What families of flavors do you notice? Does the rum mostly remind you of fruit? Of flowers? Perhaps you notice spicy, herbal, or earthy and mineral components. Does the front of your tongue detect any sweetness?

- A rum's structure should complement its flavor and bouquet. We want a big-boned rum to have a penetrating bouquet and a blockbuster flavor, and we want subtle aromas and tastes to go along with a delicate mouth feel. We sense instinctively when one of these three properties is out of proportion.

- Does the rum smell like it tastes? Flavor and bouquet should be similar, both in intensity and character. The rum should seem like a well-balanced whole. Some highly aromatic rums are disappointingly flat or annoyingly harsh in the mouth.

Think of the rum as a cylinder going through your palate from first sniff to finish. You want the rum to be the same size all the way through. By the way, this is also a useful perspective for tasting wine and beer.

- Finally, consider your whole impression of the rum from first look and sniff all the way through to the finish. Imagine it like a story or a symphony with a beginning, middle, and end. Some rums may leave you with a short, peculiar little finish or be all nose, no taste. The best rums tell a good story all the way through.

Vocabulary

You need words to describe all of this. The words are necessary because we can't conjure up images of smells or tastes without them. It's a lot like learning to appreciate any profound sensory or artistic experience: we stumble around trying to name what we experience only to find that the names actually help us experience more.

Understandable as the impulse to make up a vocabulary is, rum talk (like wine talk) is still inherently weird. We don't have a lot of words to describe tastes apart from words that give examples of similar tastes. So:

"It tastes like strawberries."
"Oh? What do strawberries taste like?"
"Sort of like this."

This is perfectly circular and takes us nowhere fast, so people reach. If they don't have words for taste, maybe they can borrow another set of words, and the next thing you know, a rum is being described as "amusing in its impudence but clearly unfocused" or something almost as silly.

But people want to talk about the stuff they drink, and one curious phenomenon helps them do it. The taste of rum creates for some of us a visual and physical impression. It's easy to say that a rum is "heavy" or "light" and most people will know what you mean. We also seem to understand intuitively the difference between a "big" rum and a "little" one. This isn't exactly the same thing as the synesthesia we discussed earlier, but it's not that different either.

A rum in balance suggests roundness, and you hear that word used a lot. You may have already tasted a rum that you found "sharp." Or perhaps there wasn't much rum in your rum and you found it "thin," "stingy," or "empty."

Now it's easy to see how this vocabulary of structure could, in the hands of a playful person, get extended a bit. Let your imagination run and try to imagine the rums that might be described as follows:

"an explosion in the candy factory"
"bewitching"
"short and mean"
"brawny"
"vivacious"

At the end, the final best tasting note is probably a simple "yes" or "no." Do you want to taste this again or not? In the case of rum, there's one further refinement: what's this rum for? (See, A Purist and A Modernist Walk into a Bar.) If the rum is to be enjoyed in a snifter with nothing more than a splash of water and some good conversation, the demands are pretty high: you want elegance and power, you want harmony, a great bouquet, and a long, elegant finish. You may have some other preferences too: some tasters dote on sugarcane, molasses, and caramel, others prefer orange and spice notes.

On the other hand, if you're thinking about cocktails, then the rum is an ingredient and your job is to harvest the desirable qualities of a rum and add them to your pantry. You may want nothing more than the bite of alcohol or you may want the extra dimensions of spice and cane.

The Taste of the Times

Having your own opinion takes time and work. That's right—there's nothing natural about it at all. In the meantime, it's nice to know that a zillion rum tasters before you have paid thoughtful attention to the matter of quality in rum. As you learn to trust your own taste, it's nice to know that there's a current consensus about what makes a good rum.

The consensus is not eternal. It changes slowly with a major fashion cycle about every two hundred years or so. The first rums were probably pretty harsh, their only grace notes coming from the time they spent in the barrels in which they were shipped. The introduction of column stills in 1830 provoked a sudden shift to a taste for more refined spirits. The minor cycles, with shifts in preference for a little more or less sweet or tannin are probably twenty- to thirty-year affairs. That said, here is the grave but slowly changing wisdom of our rum-drinking ancestors:

- A rum should have a well-defined and attractive bouquet. It should remind you that its raw material is sugarcane—not table sugar or brown sugar, but the tall, grassy, fibrous stuff that looks a little like bamboo and tastes a bit like vanilla.

- The body, or sensation of thickness in your mouth, should be proportional to the flavor and aroma; big flavors should have a heavy body, delicate ones a thin body.
- The alcohol should be detectable but not overly intrusive, seductive but not vulgar. We don't want our booze to be too boozy.
- The finish should linger in your mouth and echo the flavor of the rum. Some authors would say that the finish should remind you of the tropics, of that band of earth twenty degrees north and south of the equator where sugarcane grows. (Of course for many of us, the smell of the tropics involves sunscreen and insect repellant, but let's try to stay romantic here.)

So what flavors might you look for? Here's one checklist:

Brown sugar, vanilla, molasses, caramel, fruit, dried fruit (raisin, apricot, prune), cinnamon, spices, nutmeg, tobacco, coconut, toasted coconut, bananas, caramel, honey, chocolate, orange peel, apple, coffee, cocoa, tobacco, sherry, pepper, grass, smoke, toffee, treacle.

Some questions arise:

- When we talk about "taste," are we really talking about "smell?" Can you think of examples to the contrary?
- Why swirl?
- Isn't quality just a matter of taste? Is your taste anything more than a product of your times and social circle? What tastes will your great-grandchildren love?

- Is there anything you might learn from tasting rum that would be relevant to the rest of your life?
- What do the concepts of "balance" and "harmony" mean when applied to rum?

CHAPTER 5

WHAT DOES DRINKING MEAN?

> **The sway of alcohol over mankind is unquestionably due to its power to stimulate the mystical faculties of human nature, usually crushed to earth by the cold facts and dry criticisms of the sober hour.**
>
> *—William James*

O f course, William James missed the sixties. If he had managed a preternaturally long life span, he might have noticed that, by the twenty-first century, the "mystical faculties," rather than being uniformly "crushed to earth" often end up being screenplays, novels, and high-tech start-up companies.

> **Alcohol is a colorless, volatile, flammable liquid. It is lighter than water and a great deal more popular.**

There are two reasons that drinks with alcohol have been so loved for so long:

- The first and least obvious is that it was the only safe drink on which early civilized humankind could rely. There were simply no alternatives. A large sedentary population pollutes its own streams and ground water; deadly typhoid and cholera bacteria thrived in drinking water. Milk was unreliable and for many adults, indigestible. Fruit juice, in the days before preservatives, was either turned to vinegar through the action of bacteria or turned itself to wine by fermenting on its own yeasts. It stopped being fruit juice the minute it came into being. Only wine, which does not support any harmful bacteria and beer, which was heated as it was made, were safe. Civilizations that developed wine-making and brewing were healthier than those that did not. You might say that Natural Selection favored alcohol's entry into a part of the human diet and favored its success.

In places where the grape vines didn't grow, a heated extract of sprouted barley grains was used. (In places too cold for grapes or grain, honey in water was a substitute.) The boiling made the drink safer than the water from which it was made. Sprouted barley, sometimes called malt, contains a fair amount of starch. It also contains an enzyme that converts the starch to sugar. Soaking sprouted grain dissolves the enzyme, which attacks the starch and produces sugar. Leave that grain-sugar water out in the open air and it will be attacked by yeast and turned into beer.

- Wine was also used, in conjunction with honey, as an antiseptic in the treatment of wounds and as a medicine in itself. Hippocrates, the father of medicine in the West, prescribed it 2500 years ago for fevers, as a diuretic, and as a restorative.

The connection of wine, spirits, and beer with health remains strong today. Drinking water is still suspect in many places. (With a few exceptions, potable municipal water supplies did not appear until the seventeenth century. It was also that century that saw the introduction of the stimulant alternatives to alcohol: coffee, tea, and chocolate.) More importantly, many people connect the moderate consumption of wine and beer with a healthy and civilized life. We raise our glasses and say "to your health." Even more ambitiously, we may say "to life."

There is good evidence that these toasts are more than wishful thinking.

Of course there are other technologies that could have possibly sanitized the beverage supply, and of course the ancient Indo-Europeans knew about some of them. Wine-making and beer-brewing triumphed over all the others for reasons that had nothing to do with sanitation.

Alcohol remains popular even in the face of competition from other drinks. The reason, of course, is that alcohol has a mild and pleasantly intoxicating effect. Classical physicians like Hippocrates and Galen might have recommended wine as a medicine for various ailments, but it was Socrates who, as Hugh Johnson reminds us, commended its ability to "lull the cares of the mind to rest and . . . pleasantly invite us to agreeable mirth."

Alcohol is the anesthesia by which we endure the operation of life.

—George Bernard Shaw

It's not merely a question of medicine. Alcohol is also an ally of art. No less a figure than the brilliant Adam Gopnik has observed that ". . . it's impossible to turn the past pages of [*The New Yorker Magazine*], or the pages of American literary history, for that matter, without being reminded of how inextricable the drinking life and the writing life—or, to put it more bluntly, alcoholism and art—once were."

Gopnik, by the way, is the one who pointed out that "rumination" is but a couple of space-bar taps away from "rumination." He's also responsible for the observation that writers like an inherently unbalanced life—isolated and cerebral—and that alcohol restores a balance. Unfortunately, Gopnik doesn't tell us how that might work, but like a lot of talk about drink, his formulation sounds plausible if you say it quickly enough.

So you're reading a book about rum. Chances are that you've read a book about wine or one about beer. You're a boozy sort then, the kind of person who makes a study of his or her own weaknesses.

Or perhaps, more pathetically, you've written a book about rum. Chances are then that you've written a book about wine and maybe even another about beer. You're a boozy sort then, the kind of person who makes a point of mouthing off about his or her own weaknesses.

Let's close the doors here.

"Hello, my name is Lynn and I really like alcohol."

"Hi, Lynn."

"Alcohol is my friend. Chances are that if you're in this meeting, alcohol is pretty important to you too. I'll even bet that you have a few books around your house about drinks that owe some of their charm to alcohol. Maybe you even have some booze-toys: a wine fridge, a bench-mounted corkscrew, home-brewing equipment, a wine cellar, special drinking glasses."

Mumble, murmur. . .

"Wait, there's more. I'll bet that you've had five good ideas and fifteen bad ones while you were drinking. I'll even bet that some of those ideas did you a lot of good and—maybe—that some did you a bit of harm. Sound familiar?"

Murmur, chair scrape.

"It does? Good, let's talk."

Epicureanism

If you're a subscriber to *Wine Spectator* or a reader of the Short Course series, there's a good chance that you've been accused at some point or other of being nothing more than a common drunk.

Getting High

If you've experienced the slight elevation of mood, the balmy driftiness that comes with a drink or two, there's a good chance that you've also from time to time thought that something you were drinking was uncommonly delicious, maybe even divinely so. Perhaps you've become interested in the stuff you drink, maybe you even have learned conversations.

> **"Drinking is an emotional thing. It joggles you out of the standardism of everyday life, out of everything being the same. It yanks you out of your body and your mind and throws you against the wall. I have the feeling that drinking is a form of suicide where you're allowed to return to life and begin all over the next day. It's like killing yourself, and then you're reborn. I guess I've lived about ten or fifteen thousand lives now."**
> —*Charles Bukowski*

Drink Hates Those Who Love It Most

If you were to look for a poster child for Ambivalence, you couldn't do better than to take the ancient, revered,

reviled, celebrated, castigated custom of enjoying drinks
with alcohol. The ambivalence is built in. Oooh look:
there's the "mystical faculties" (all of them) along with
the pathetic drunk and domestic violence and hideous
car accident, all sitting at a table together.
I wonder who's the Master of Ceremonies tonight.

Of the approximately 200 million people who drink rum, only a few are Bukowskis or Hemingways. The proportion doesn't go up when you include other beverage alcohol or even other drugs. Drink is there because it soothes, because it dresses a wound: maybe boredom, maybe loneliness, certainly pain.

Alcohol's other virtue is that it has a mild and pleasantly intoxicating effect. One of the first questions people ask about rum is its (alcoholic) "strength." What a peculiar expression! You might want to know how many milligrams of salt are in your soup or the amount of cholesterol in your salad dressing, but when it comes to alcohol, you ask "how strong?" Is that a measure of respect or an acknowledgement of fear?

Well, the general answer is easy. When measured by volume, most rum is between 40 and 50 percent alcohol. In the United States all distilled spirits are required to put their "strength" right out there on the label.

The alcohol in any beverage comes from the sugar. In the case of rum the sugar is derived from molasses, the by-product of sugar refining. The more sugar you start out with, the more there is for the yeast to consume and the more alcohol you'll have when you're done. From there, it's simply a matter of deciding how much water you're going to remove from the alcohol and water mixture. It's worth noting that since alcohol is much lighter than water, the question of "how much alcohol" has two different answers.

The first answer is a matter of percentage of alcohol by weight, and is the one preferred by brewers and distillers for its direct relation to the distillation process and its ease of calculation. A gram of sugar yields about half a gram of alcohol. The second answer is by the percentage of the total volume and is preferred by collectors of the excise tax. It's also the one that appears on rum bottle labels as ALC/VOL. To calculate the percentage by volume, just multiply the percentage by weight by 1.25.

There is a move afoot to require distillers to put nutritional information labels on their bottles. You probably already know that rum isn't particularly rich in vitamin B1, has no fat and no fiber. Also zero protein and none of the common allergens.

So who's behind this? On one side is a neo-prohibitionist outfit called the Center for Science in the Public Interest. Allied with them is Diageo, owner of the Guinness brand and some of the most prestigious distilled spirits in the world. CSPI is hoping, according to a spokesman, "to reduce the problems associated with drinking." Diageo, on the other hand, uses its website to promote parity between spirits and beer: same alcohol, different vehicles. Apparently this spirits giant feels that a statement about the "equivalence" of beer and spirits will be to the advantage of spirits. Beer has been making strange bedfellows for years, but this pairing is remarkable: one side hopes to decrease consumption of alcohol, the other is trying to increase it. Somebody's going to look gullible here. Stay tuned.

What you probably do want to know is: how many calories are there in rum? One ounce of 80 proof (40 percent ALC/VOL) white rum has 64 calories, all of them from alcohol which itself has 7 calories per ounce. Higher proof rums will have proportionally more calories and darker rums (which may have a bit of sugar added) may have a bit more. Adding 8 ounces of coke (96 calories) to your one ounce of rum, yields a drink with 160 calories.

Alcohol and the Human Body

Alcohol gets into the your body from all parts of the gastrointestinal tract largely by simple diffusion into the blood; however, the small intestine is by far the most efficient region of the gastrointestinal tract for alcohol absorption because of its very large surface area. Alcohol is absorbed into your bloodstream and forwarded on to your brain through tissues in your mouth, stomach, and small intestine. Alcohol in the blood quickly travels throughout the body.

Alcohol and the Brain

Alcohol affects the brain with a strict attention to the class system. The aristocratic neighborhoods—the Rittenhouse Squares of your skull—get beat up first. Judgment—as you may have heard—becomes impaired. Sensory information gets scrambled, thinking gets, um, disordered, and then voluntary muscular movements become a tidge uncoordinated.

After the inner philosopher is trashed, alcohol moves on to rough up the poet. People become subject to exaggerated emotions and memory loss. Delicacy of feeling is a casualty. With your inner Billy Collins dead and gone, more alcohol (that is, a higher concentration in the blood) goes after the animal inside you.

You know that test where they ask you to close your eyes and touch your finger to your nose? The ability that's being tested is mediated through a part of your brain called the cerebellum and you can usually do it smoothly. (If you haven't had a drink in a few hours, try it now. Easy, no?) Turn off the cerebellum—as that extra drink will do—and the movements become jerky and uncertain (as do you). These delicate movements are like the ones that we use to control our balance, and so the cerebellum-pickled drinker may start falling down.

The lusty animal is affected too. Alcohol depresses the areas of the hypothalamus that coordinate sexual endocrine functions. So although sexual behavior may increase, sexual performance declines. In men, this is the so-called "whisky-dick" effect.

If for some reason, you get to this point and still manage to keep on drinking, you may be saved by the body's natural tendency to fall asleep. This tendency is also referred to less kindly as passing out, and indulging in it more than once can get you banned from some very nice taverns. It can also make you subject to the worst impulses of your fellow drinkers.

If Morpheus—Sleep God, Brother of Death—doesn't come to your rescue, or if you manage to bypass him by swallowing a flood of alcohol in a very short time, then breathing, heart rate, and body temperature centers are affected. Blood pressure can drop and breathing can stop and your organ donor card and emergency instructions may be invoked. Be aware that drinking yourself to death gives the rest of us a bad name.

Getting Rid of it

Fortunately, the same body that took all that alcohol in is capable of hauling it out, mostly by oxidizing it in the liver. A small amount is expelled in the breath, saliva, urine, feces, and sweat. (A small amount is also excreted in breast milk, although if you're producing breast milk and drinking lots of alcohol, perhaps you should be reading some other book.) Except for the possible acceleration caused by jumping into a sauna or running a marathon, most of us eliminate alcohol at a steady rate.

There is some variability among people in their ability to metabolize and get rid of what they paid to take in. This ability is sometimes called "holding your liquor" although in fact, it's really more like the ability to let it go. The big differences between people are the water content and fat content of the body. Here's what you should know:

- The less you weigh, the more you will be affected by a given amount of alcohol. Bigger people have more blood and more tissue and so the alcohol is diluted over a larger volume.

- The more muscular you are, the less affected you'll be. Fat doesn't have much water (duh), and muscular souls have more blood vessels and more water-absorbing tissue. Don't try to outdrink the power-lifters or the body-builders.

- Gender counts. Women have a triple whammy here. They tend to have smaller bodies with higher body fat percentages, which means less watery tissue. They also tend to process alcohol through the liver more slowly because of a lower level of an alcohol-digesting hormone.

- Age matters too. Older people eliminate alcohol more slowly, although the effects of this may be mitigated by the so-called "practice effect." This is part of what's behind the common observation that old drunks can handle their liquor better. It has been suggested too, that old drunks are merely the survivors of a culling process. Further research is called for.

- Food can slow the absorption of alcohol through several mechanisms. Not only is alcohol slowed in its entrance to the small intestine, but the lower concentrations of alcohol that result actually speed up the rate at which your body processes the alcohol.

There's more, of course. Arousal can slow the passage of alcohol from the stomach to the intestine and the person looking for a predetermined level of buzz may fail to reach it with the first few doses and then overshoot. Anxiety can increase the rate of absorption and so can carbonation and even artificial sweeteners. So, let's lay off the aspartame-enhanced over-proof rum when we're really, really tense, okay?

Just What Do We Mean by "Drunk"?

Alcohol that isn't metabolized in the liver remains in the blood stream. A person whose blood contains more than 0.1 percent alcohol is considered legally drunk in most jurisdictions. In many European countries, the standard for judging a driver to be "under the influence of alcohol" is much lower—in Italy and Austria, it's just half the American threshhold. In Japan, any alcohol at all in a driver's blood is illegal and passengers in the car are also subject to fines. These specific numbers are necessary for the law and reassuring to the rest of us. Over this line lies "drunk".

Some of us may have also some personal experience of the matter-studied it in our own phenomenology lab, let's say. It's not surprising that we end up thinking that we know exactly what "drunk" is.

But drunkenness is far from a single, simple thing. It's a continuum that involves emotions, perception, consciousness, and behavior. At one end of the scale is a pleasant lightening of the spirit, the sort of uplift that has made the drink after work a ritual and the glass of wine before dinner a necessity for so many. At the other end, there is the disastrous breakdown of all the human functions: the blithering, destructive wreck.

In between, there are an infinite number of states along each of those dimensions: some of the combinations are pleasant, others exalted, and some others purely miserable. As any bartender or cocktail waitress can tell you, a person drunk can be remarkably different from that same person sober, and there are many, many different ways for a person to be drunk.

The shift from sober to drunk may be as drastic to the person undergoing it as it is to the outsider watching him or her. Shy people become outgoing, timid folks become foolhardy, inhibited souls discover their libidinous side. If drunkenness were not such a common experience and one so often depicted, we would be astonished by it and beg for an explanation.

Whenever we try to explain inebriation we're immediately confronted with questions about the idea of explanation itself. In fact we may end up with more questions about causality than with answers about being drunk. A glib explanation of drunkeness is that people get drunk because alcohol disinhibits the brain. Does this explain it? Not hardly. Unless you have a deep understanding of brain physiology, that's just another set of words for the same thing. (You might as easily say that the rum bunny came along and replaced your brain with a Waring blender, or that you were possessed by a god.)

This sounds great and grave but it's really just circular thinking. Looking for a cause? Give the effect a different name. What causes loneliness? No friends! What causes poverty? No money! We're easily duped into accepting this sort of circular thinking as an explanation because, as citizens of our own times, we have a certain faith in the material dimension of things. So we think that by restating the question with a reference to something more concrete or measureable, we've "explained" it. We're right go in that direction: rigorous material explanations make for good engineering. But before this belief came along in, let's say the seventeenth century, what kind of explanation might have occurred to people who wondered just what drunkenness was?

Forget what you know for a minute, and imagine that you're drinking some alcohol-enhanced drink for the first time. Let's say that you live in a world with few physical comforts and a badly stocked medicine chest. What would it be like to get drunk for the first time? For most people, drinking probably just lessened the daily dose of pain and made them feel less bad. (Quick: imagine your world without aspirin or dentistry or any of the patent medicines in that chest above your sink.) Anyway, this "feeling good" must have seemed like a surprise visit to another place, a divine place.

Remember, the notion of alcohol as some specific property of a drink is a fairly new idea. Distilling the "spirit" of wine only began in the thirteenth century and the word *alcohol* comes into existence thanks to Paracelsus, the physician/alchemist of Salzburg in the seventeenth century. Giving a name to the ingredient that makes one drunk created a step back, a kind of abstraction (although not, of course, an explanation.). Before that, there was only the mystery of the drink itself.

What to make of that mystery? Let's go back some more. In much of the ancient world the drink and its effect seemed like a gift from the gods. The ancient Greeks were not very fond of their gods. They (the gods, not the Greeks) were a nasty bunch. But one of them was different: Dionysus, the god of wine. He entered your body when you drank wine, you could feel his presence and his presence was a present.

But Dionysus was not completely a warm fuzzy teddy bear. The adjective "Dionysian" frequently modifies the noun "frenzy." The festivals in his honor were known for their wild dancing and uninhibited behavior.

The Greece of the classics died after Alexander, and the Romans inherited the bones if not the spirit. They also inherited important aspects of Greek drinking culture, particularly the notion of drink and its consequences as visitations from the divine.

In Rome, Dionysus becomes Bacchus, and he appears in murals and mosaics with a halo of leaves and sitting as an infant on the knee of his virgin mother, Semele.

The Greeks built their civilization on the trade in wine, and Romans, like modern Italians, were wine-drinkers first. Wine

A Greek slave assists a drunk diner in vomiting. Brygos Painter, 500–470 BC. Photo by Stefano Bolognini.

gods were prosperity gods. Beer had a role at the fringes of the world where grapes didn't grow. There was a Greco-Roman god of beer. He is Silenus (fat, bald, and drunk) and he makes a pointed cultural contrast to the pretty Dionysus. He is a low-rent, minor divinity but there is still no way to talk about drunk on beer except by calling up a god.

In the Egyptian world, Osiris is the god of agriculture who taught people how to brew. There is also a profound connection between the importance of beer and its inebriating effect in the story of the goddess Hathor. In a tale that parallels the story of the Flood, the god Ra punishes rebellious mankind by creating a bloodthirsty goddess, Hathor. Alarmed at the extent of her destruction and taking pity on mankind, he orders beer to be brewed and mixed with red ochre and uses it to flood the place where Hathor is to continue her killing. The murderous goddess sees the lake of blood:

> Then she laughed with joy, and her laughter was like the roar of a lioness hungry for the kill. Thinking that it was indeed blood, she stooped and drank. Again and yet again she drank, laughing with delight; and the strength of the beer mounted to her brain, so that she could no longer slay.
>
> At last she came reeling back to where Ra was waiting; that day she had not killed even a single man.
>
> Then Ra said: "You come in peace, sweet one." And her name was changed to Hathor, and her nature was changed also to the sweetness of love and the strength of desire. And henceforth Hathor laid low men and women only with the great power of love. But forever after her priestesses drank in her honor of the beer of Heliopolis colored with the red ochre of Elephantine when they celebrated her festival each New Year.

In the story, the power of the beer is that it turns wrath into love. Even the mushy sentimentality of drunks has a divine origin.

Alcohol and Attitude

There are some people who hate alcohol for its virtues. These are folks who are threatened by that lighter, looser state of consciousness in themselves and other people, the fear that the jolly poet is really the lecherous pirate in disguise. One person's lightened spirit becomes someone else's terrorizing demon. You probably don't need me to tell you that people drinking rum—

or anything else—are more likely to be boisterous and to act out sexually.

Ask anyone who's ever tended a bar or cleaned up after a drunk: alcohol may have gods, but it is not always a blessing. Sitting at the same table with the lightened spirits and occasional hilarity of good-natured drinking sits the destructive nightmare of the out-of-control drunk.

Those people drinking rum are also more likely to be aggressive, obnoxious, or deficient in good judgment. The worst of it is summed up in the Hogarth engraving *Gin Lane*.

Gin Lane is the artist William Hogarth's vision of the effects of hard liquor (in this case, gin) on the people of London. He contrasted this with the happy and virtuous folks on Beer Street.

All culture is built on some sort of inhibition, and if your idea of goodness is based on a heavy-duty set of inhibitions, then the moderately disinhibiting effect of alcohol is likely to be very threatening. People who have come to be afraid of their own impulses are often also repelled by them and find themselves wanting to wipe out or at least disguise those impulses in others. Alcohol is an enemy of inhibitions and therefore an enemy to the inhibited, which is, on some level, all of us.

A really personal understanding of alcohol starts with acknowledging the feelings, attitudes, and knowledge that you bring to your glass of rum. These are the feelings you acquired at home, think of them as Mom and Dad. After you own up to those feelings, it's good to remember where we're doing our

No account of the pleasures of drinking can sidestep the question of the horror caused by drunken drivers. According to the Centers for Disease Control, over 17,000 people died in alcohol-related automobile accidents in 2007. (Almost 30,000 people were killed by guns that same year.)

In spite of the fact that almost three-quarters of those convicted of drunk driving violations are alcoholics, it's a bad idea for anyone to mix even moderate alcohol consumption and driving. Designated drivers and good public transit systems are a drinker's best friends. If you have a choice, drink beer in Vienna, rum in Havana, wine in Rome, and bottled water in Los Angeles.

drinking. In America, we're still pretty much car-crazy. In more tolerant contexts, people more frequently walk from place to place. A certain unsteadiness on the street may be amusing, but the same impairment at the wheel can be deadly.

In the United States, alcohol is the subject of much passionate debate and very little rational reflection. By some estimates, a third of American adults do not drink any drink that contains alcohol. For some it is a matter of religious belief: Mormons, Muslims, and Hindus do not drink. Members of some Christian sects construe even the wine-friendly Bible as forbidding drinking. In addition, there are millions of people who believe that their personal problems have their roots in an uncontrollable addiction to alcohol. This last group has brewed up a large "alcoholism industry." Look up the word "Alcoholism" in an American phone directory and you will see a list of organizations that derive their reason for being from the perception of alcohol as a threat.

On the other hand (there is always, in discussion of alcohol, an other hand), recent studies have shown with an amazing regularity that people who drink beer and wine moderately and regularly are physically and emotionally healthier in every sense than those who drink too little or those who drink too much. These research results get a lot less publicity than do the dueling, contradictory, and less useful results of studies about the health effects of other foods. Results showing the benign effects of drinking have, of course, been deliberately ignored by the alcoholism industry.

In the face of all this high-key and often very primitive passion, it is sometimes difficult for reasonable voices to be heard. (Let's record that sentence: let's use it as a ringtone on our iPhone.) Tolerance and moderation are inherently less spectacular than absolutism. In the matter of alcohol, as in so many other matters, Tolerance and Patience are the two virtues that count.

Here's another shocker: for many college students, being at least nominally on their own for the first time and having virtually unlimited access to alcoholic beverages for the first time gives rise to some pretty crazy behavior. What's at the heart of it is that many students have no experience of drinking alcohol as a part of a moderate enjoyment. It's always easy for the grownups on a college campus to tell who grew up in a family of moderate drinkers and who didn't. The kids who drink moderately are smiling on Monday morning: the apprentice drunks and the glumly abstemious are not. If excess drinking only cost the occasional freshman hangover, we could pass over college drunkenness as a mere rite of passage. But in fact, even in the Eden of college life, immoderate drinking can exact a very high price. Unwanted pregnancy, STDs, date rape, fatal accidents, and other calamities can all be the outcome of too much alcohol.

So how does a person learn moderation? The best advice I ever heard for novice drinkers was wonderfully simple: Drink like you've been doing it all your life and like you will be doing it forever. Imagine that it's fun and tasty and no big deal, and then it will be. For the parents of kids who are not yet drinking, the best advice I ever heard was: Show your kids what moderation looks like and you'll never have to tell them. For college administrators, the best advice might be to provide high-profile occasions on which moderate drinking is the norm. My genteel old alma mater used to host a "Dean's tea" every semester for everyone who made Dean's List. It was an afternoon event and everyone, faculty, deans, and students alike had a glass or two of sherry. It almost seemed like real life.

Moderation

In case you hadn't noticed, unrestricted drinking and drunkenness have fallen out of favor at the same time that wine columns are appearing in suburban newspapers and artisanal rums are showing up in liquor stores. We find ourselves with a shrill and uneasy battle between people of good will holding these two positions:

- Drinking is Death! Drinking any drink with alcohol in it is sinful or unhealthy or irresponsible. Drinkers are hurting themselves and threatening the rest of us. In fact, any explicit attempt to control the nature of one's own consciousness subverts natural law and true religion.
- Drinking is Life! Drinking is fun and one person's drinking is none of anyone else's business. The government is not entitled to tax or regulate one person's pleasures more punitively than another's.

Unlike most of our dichotomies, these two positions are distributed across a range of political beliefs and economic circumstance. There are progressives and conservatives on both sides of that line, rich and poor distributed in both camps.

Notice that neither position is particularly moderate. But let's not rush to pronounce an anathema on either or both of these camps. Moderation is a Johnny-come-lately virtue, a habit that has to be learned and that has no great tradition behind it. In fact moderate drinking is a recent and necessary next step in human development.

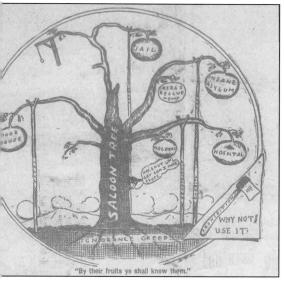

"By their fruits ye shall know them."

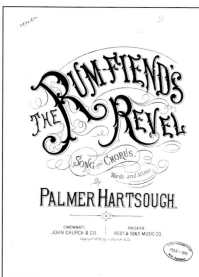

Two dim pre-prohibition views of rum.

Why drink moderately? Because there is really no sane alternative. Unrestricted drunkenness may have been a scandal in the seventeenth century; in our times it's dangerous and intolerable. The drunk in George II's England could start a fight, perhaps kill somebody. Today's drunk can pass out at the switch of the power plant or careen down the freeway and take out a school bus.

If unrestricted drinking is unthinkable, so is Prohibition in both its disguised and blatant forms. If America's disastrous experience described above was not enough to prove the point, one could turn to the British Gin Act of 1736, which managed to quadruple the consumption of locally distilled gin in a mere seven years by prohibiting the import of liquor.

More important than that is the fact that drinks with alcohol add to the civilized pleasures of a world without much civilization and with precious little pleasure. Prohibitionists are

THE AMERICAN ISSUE

A Saloonless Nation and a Stainless Flag

Volume XXVI   WESTERVILLE, OHIO, JANUARY 25, 1919   Number 4

U.S. IS VOTED DRY

36th STATE RATIFIES DRY AMENDMENT JAN. 16

Nebraska Noses Out Missouri for Honor of Completing Job of Writing Dry Act Into the Constitution; Wyoming, Wisconsin and Minnesota Right on Their Heels

JANUARY 16, 1919, MOMENTOUS DAY IN WORLD'S HISTORY

trying to take their lack of culture and their joylessness out on the rest of us. It may also be worth noting that there is no real opposite of Prohibitionism apart from Moderation. The radical Drys have no counterpart on the other side.

Moderation is not only sound policy, it is good sense too. The medical evidence is overwhelming: moderate enjoyment of drinks with alcohol adds to a healthy life. But drinking without getting drunk only makes sense if the drinking is a reward in itself. Fine rum is a drink of moderation because it's delicious. We'll have some practical advice about moderation later, but for now let's just note that good rum (and good wine and good beer) make moderation as pleasant as it is virtuous.

Moderation and Ambivalence

These observations about alcohol and moderation are not exactly new. They seem to have been dueling almost as long as alcohol has been around, although the debate heats up as more potent

Districts.	Whisky.	Rum.	Gin.	High wines.	Alcohol.	Neutral or cologne spirits.	Aggregate.
DISTILLERY WAREHOUSES.							
Alabama	21,677.7		1,317.4				22,995.1
1st California			1,572.1		303,201.2	2,584.8	307,358.1
Connecticut			10,822.4				10,822.4
Hawaii		939.2	2,002.5		1,863.5		4,805.2
1st Illinois	13,730.5				30,062.7	92.5	43,885.7
5th Illinois	5,610,074.0		913,218.4		1,037,462.9	2,411,583.6	9,972,338.9
8th Illinois	1,581,243.2		27,936.4		102,378.5	571,610.7	2,283,168.8
6th Indiana	2,884,624.9		116,778.3		186,002.7	228,564.7	3,415,970.6
7th Indiana	1,178,712.6		253,468.4		87,267.3	1,149,965.3	2,669,413.6
2d Kentucky	11,265,745.2				53,954.0		11,319,699.2
5th Kentucky	41,155,333.7		79,790.9		373,287.1		41,608,411.7
6th Kentucky	6,823,100.8	26,475.5	169,465.7	1,122.3	10,283.6		7,030,447.9
7th Kentucky	16,502,653.2		101,948.1			91,915.5	16,696,516.8
8th Kentucky	9,865,459.0						9,865,459.0
Louisiana			29,928.9		1,409,951.8	389,061.3	1,828,942.0
Maryland	11,404,726.9		19,819.2		3,292,091.4		14,716,637.5
3d Massachusetts		700,835.8	6,407.5		477,463.6		1,184,706.9
1st Michigan					2,836.8	167,547.0	170,383.8
1st Missouri	172,172.1						172,172.1
6th Missouri	280,008.0						280,008.0
Montana	9,530.3				2,748.1		12,278.4
1st New York			41,457.8		151,713.7	35,167.7	228,339.2
14th New York	528,658.1		677,947.3		33,695.4	82.3	1,240,383.1
21st New York	309,993.3		54,388.5	631.6	588.2	213,520.5	579,122.1
28th New York	9,416.0						9,416.0
1st Ohio	6,564,402.9		202,104.3	909.6	55,419.9	524,849.2	7,347,685.9
11th Ohio	1,176.2						1,176.2
18th Ohio	201,586.9						201,586.9
1st Pennsylvania	1,765,084.4			929.3	86,382.8	50,262.8	1,902,659.3
9th Pennsylvania	797,679.5						797,679.5
12th Pennsylvania	85,811.3						85,811.3
23d Pennsylvania	19,960,914.7		1,077.6	7,303.7		28,012.7	19,997,308.7
South Carolina					15,670.5		15,670.5
3d Texas					10,798.9		10,798.9
6th Virginia	15,859.6						15,859.6
West Virginia	453,806.5						453,806.5
1st Wisconsin	157,523.6		15,278.2		43,484.4	823.2	217,109.4
Total	139,620,705.1	728,250.5	2,726,729.9	10,896.5	7,768,609.0	5,865,643.8	156,720,834.8
GENERAL BONDED WAREHOUSES.							
1st California	535,028.4	10,911.0	20,193.9		77,770.1	199,933.4	843,836.8
6th California	79,063.5	303.0	2,695.9		15,226.4	11,970.4	109,259.2
Hawaii					279.2		279.2
5th Kentucky	112,749.7	371.4	6,456.1		140,291.1		259,868.3
6th Missouri	117,065.7	1,268.3	4,836.2		66,715.4	24,156.1	214,041.7
1st Ohio	136,931.7		5,249.6		12,908.7	133,991.8	289,081.8
Oregon					12,075.2	8,805.1	20,880.3
2d Virginia	15,777.2						15,777.2
1st Pennsylvania	104,500.2		11,306.1		4,504.6	365,094.3	485,405.2
Total	1,101,116.4	12,853.7	50,737.8	000.0	329,770.7	743,951.1	2,238,429.7
Grand total	140,721,821.5	741,104.2	2,777,467.7	10,896.5	8,098,379.7	6,609,594.9	158,959,264.5

On 1918, on the eve of Prohibition, rum accounted for less than one-half of 1 percent of all distilled spirits consumed in the United States, but the dry crusade was still about Demon Rum.

alcoholic drinks become available in the 1600s. In a few societies, one point of view has temporarily overridden the other, but the most common condition has been a kind of armed truce between the two views and the people who represent them. One American writer saw the thing clearly:

RUM, n. Generically, fiery liquors that produce madness in total abstainers."
—Ambrose Bierce

If you want to play search-a-quote, you can assemble similar pairs of epigrams from many other cultures.

Two things are obvious after the beer lovers and the naysayers have been heard from:

- The rum lovers have all the good lines:

"There's naught, no doubt, so much the spirit calms as rum and true religion."
—Lord Byron

"There can't be good living where there is not good drinking."
—Benjamin Franklin

"I have taken more out of alcohol than alcohol has taken out of me."
—Winston Churchill

- The "solution" that most thinkers recommend is the middle ground of moderation:

"Drink the first. Sip the second slowly. Skip the third."

—Knute Rockne

So what's moderate? What we want is a way to enjoy the deliciousness and the voluptuosity of drinking without becoming a sad casualty of it. The real question is "how much?": The Attic Greeks specified three drinks as the righteous dose: the first for health, the second for companionship, and the third for sleep. For us spiritual descendants of the Attic Greeks, the standard of moderation is one drink an hour. We'll define a drink as twelve ounces of 5 percent beer, five ounces of wine, or an ounce of rum.

Coincidentally, that one drink an hour is about the rate at which your above-mentioned liver can reduce alcohol to sugar. Anything above that, remember, goes into your blood and brain as alcohol. It's this "excess" alcohol spilling out of an overworked liver that makes us drunk. One drink is, with food, a fairly civilized pace of consumption. One might even call it moderate.

PROHIBITION TODAY

The impulse to smack a foaming fragrant glass out of someone's hand is not dead. In the western world, it is nowadays less likely to be advocated by a preacher and more likely to come from a nutritionist.

The Bottom Line

Rum has alcohol and alcohol has a central and powerful place in the imaginations of most people. It's a reason we drink rum and a reason that we don't. It is the devil and it is a god, the food of angels and madmen. It is the source of tremendous benefits and we pay a fairly high price for them. It is easy to love alcohol and only a bit harder to hate it.

Somewhere between those two extremes there's a place where we recognize that the good or evil in things may not be in the things themselves, but in us. That's a place called moderation.

CHAPTER 6

RUM
RECIPES

Rum stands alone among distilled spirits when it comes to cooking. Rum partakes of the sweet, the fragrant, the harsh, the smooth, and the dry. You can evoke fire or sunshine. The presence of rum as an ingredient in food is so intense that it can be considered as important as the power of rum as a drink.

For many of us, there's no purer rum dessert than the magnificent and excessive baba au rhum. It's a yeast-raised spongy cake that's soaked—I mean saturated—in sweetened rum. It's eaten wetly with a fork or a spoon and the rich caramel/vanilla and penetrating nose of the spirit provides the flavor spike that enlivens the cake. Most rum-based dishes rely on the same trick: caramel and vanilla are great friends of sweetness, throw 'em together and you can't go wrong.

There's another contribution that rum can make in the kitchen and that's in the earthy edge it gives to meats and stews. If you have a dish to which you could conceivably add maple syrup, brown sugar, or any sweetened sauce, it could probably benefit from a touch of rum.

When in Doubt, Flambé

Once upon a time, before cities like Philadelphia, Madrid, and San Francisco became the centers of ambitious, delicious food, the world looked meekly to Paris and Lyons for the techniques and recipes that excited the imagination if not the palate. One of the most dramatic techniques was the relatively simple matter of dousing a food with a high-proof alcohol and setting it on fire.

Rum is a good fuel for flambé as in this Bananas Foster. Photo by Jenene Chesbrough.

The (presumably fakelore) story of its origin has a waiter in nineteenth century Monte Carlo accidently setting fire to a dish of booze-soaked crêpes that were about to be served to a visiting princeling. The flustered waiter named the dish after the fellow's companion and thus Crêpes Suzette were born.

In America, this dish survived as an expensive prom night/ seduction dinner/proposal of marriage flourish that was said to cause an entire dining room to turn its head and gasp in admiration at its sheer grandeur and profligacy. Restaurants of a certain haute bourgeois type always kept this dish or its cousin Cherries Jubilee on the menu. More ambitious places may have added the word "flambé" to a dessert item and doubled its price, thereby increasing both check size and tips for the waiter or maître d'.

Photo by Javier Lastras.

no dessert is spiced with such romance
it invites the diner to a dance,
to eat, to gorge to take a chance
to madly throw off shirt and pants.

There's passion hid in just the name
there's hints of riches, sex and fame
and so, alas, it's such a shame,
they're only flapjacks set aflame.

A Word of Caution

Setting things on fire in your dining room is a bad idea. Don't do it. If in spite of this good advice, you decide to put a match to a flammable liquid inside a building, well . . . you've been warned.

How to Flambé

Simply pouring Sterno on food and setting it afire is not flambéing. What you need is a sauce that combines alcohol, sugar, and water. Burning the alcohol changes the character of the sauce by caramelizing the sugar, removing the harsh flavor of raw alcohol, and leaving behind whatever essence the alcohol carried with it. Thus, flambéed rum leaves the tang of burnt sugar and the spiciness of the rum. Flambéed gin leaves the hint of juniper and angelica, and bourbon gives you caramel and oak.

Some recipes recommend flambéing with 151 proof rum or higher. Aside from being relatively low in residual flavor, these spirits are highly flammable and are a bad thing to have anywhere near an open flame. Rum, at 80 to 100 proof and diluted with other ingredients, is ideal.

The rum must be heated before lighting it on fire. This makes it much less likely to ignite when you don't want it to. What happens is that since alcohol has a lower boiling point than water, as you heat the mixture, the fumes of evaporating alcohol rise first. When you bring your long fireplace match close to the mixture, what ignites are the vapors above the sauce. The flame is pale and blue and in the old days, the lights were usually lowered to both dramatize and emphasize the fiery moment. Cinnamon and clove, both of which are of an oily nature, are sometimes added not only for flavor, but for show as the powder ignites when added.

So here we go. Let's start with a pan on the stove, some butter and some bananas.

Bananas Adler, *pioneered by the famous physician-gourmet Dr. Joan*
Adler

1 ounce (25 g) butter
2 tablespoons brown sugar
1 banana peeled, halved, and cut lengthwise
2 ounces (50 ml) dark rum
Vanilla ice cream
Lady fingers or homemade genoise

On a small plate, arrange the lady fingers to form a square. Scoop vanilla ice cream in the center of the square. In a small skillet, melt the butter. Use a wooden spoon so you don't burn your fingers later on when things get hot. Add the brown sugar and stir. Add the banana and cook until browned (caramelized) on both sides, over medium-high heat. Move pan off heat, add the rum and stir. Return to the stove and either tilt the pan to catch a bit of flame or use a long fireplace match to set the vapors on fire. Stand back when ignited and let the bananas brown. When the flame dies the alcohol has been cooked out. Serve bananas over vanilla ice cream and/or a slice of pound cake.

Cherries Jubilee

1 pint vanilla ice cream
1 pound (500 g) cherries, stemmed and pitted
½ cup (100 g) sugar
1 lemon
½ cup (100 ml) brown rum

The rich, complex cherry sauce will merge beautifully into a very creamy French-style vanilla ice cream or gelato. Unfortunately, it will also make a cheap, gummy ice cream seem cheaper. Choose with the angels.

Cherries Jubilee, a once-popular dessert, may be due for a comeback. Photo by Stu Spivack.

Scoop the ice cream into four dishes or decorative glasses and put in the freezer until ready to serve (this can be done up to four hours ahead).

Wash and pit the cherries. Put the cherries and sugar in a large skillet. Peel 2 strips of zest from the lemon in wide strips with a peeler and add to the cherries. Squeeze the juice of half the lemon over the top. Stir to combine evenly. Cover and cook the cherries over medium-low heat until the sugar dissolves, about 4 minutes. Uncover and cook over medium-high until cherries get juicy, about 5 minutes more.

To flambé the rum: If cooking over a gas flame, pull the pan off the heat and add the rum. Ignite the alcohol with a long match or one held with tongs. Swirl the pan slightly until the flames subside, about 30 seconds.

Wait a minute or two. Some authorities recommend a waiting period to give the cherries time to think about themselves and get ready for their big moment. Others feel that the slightly cooled cherries are less likely to crack the now-frozen glasses. After an appropriate waiting period, ladle the cherries and their juices over prepared ice cream scoops. Serve immediately.

What does all this pyromania do to the taste? There is some dispute here and that's remarkable considering how much drama is involved. Some chefs deride the whole business as sheer showmanship, others say that there is a subtle difference, and a third group maintains that the showmanship is the point. (Could you ever forget a dinner that ended with a flaming rum-soaked slice of pound cake being extinguished by a gush of whipped cream?)

Savory Dishes

Francis Hogan, executive chef at Bluestem Brasserie, San Francisco and member of the Butchers' Guild was recently honored at the James Beard House in New York. Here's his take on rum and grilled meat.

Rum Marinated Rib Eye Steak

> 4 (12 ounce) rib eye steaks
> 13 ounces white rum
> 6.5 ounces extra virgin olive oil

1/3 cup brown sugar

1 tablespoon Sriracha

2 tablespoons strong Dijon mustard

2 tablespoons kosher salt

Combine everything except the steak and whisk until sugar and salt dissolve.

Place steaks in a Ziploc bag and pour marinade over.

Marinate for 24 hours, turning the bag once.

Remove the steaks from the bag. Allow excess marinade to drip off.

Season the steaks with salt and pepper and cook as desired. Serve with chimichurri.

Chimichurri:

1 bunch Italian parsley, chopped

6 garlic cloves, minced

¾ cup extra virgin olive oil

¼ cup red wine vinegar

2 tablespoons fresh lemon juice

½ teaspoon red pepper flakes

2 teaspoons kosher salt

1 teaspoon black pepper

Stir all ingredients to combine.

Notice that Chef Hogan doesn't say what to do with the marinade. What you've got left is a bit under a pint of a sweet, sour, oily, hot, salty liquid. Chilled and covered, it will keep almost indefinitely. What can you use it for? (You'll probably want to boil the marinade to ensure that it's bacteria-free.) Here are three suggestions:

Roasted quail in rum glaze. Copyright © 2006 David Monniaux.

Deglazing

Every good cook should know this: When you brown meat, vegetables, or fish in a very hot pan, you get two products. You get the browned food itself and also its footprint, bits of brown that stick to the pan. These brownings are the most thoroughly transformed, caramelized essences of the food itself and it's a pity to rinse them down the drain when you wash the pan. Instead, lower the heat and add some liquid, stirring to dissolve the brownings. If you use a flavorful liquid like wine or beer, you're on your way to a light, simple sauce. Add a bit of vinegar

The simplest sauce.

to the wine and you have the elegant, lively accent called a gastrique. Or you can add a bit of Hogan's Marinade and have a wonderfully complex sauce that complements a range of meats and fishes. If you think of the appeal of barbecue, you've got it. Sifting a bit of ultra-fine flour into the liquid as it heats in the pan gives you a thicker sauce. Adding rum, allowing it to begin to vaporize and then setting the vapors on fire is a savory extension of the flambé technique we discussed earlier.

Salad or Vegetable Dressing

Salad greens and most vegetables rely on a simple flavor or two and a crisp texture for their appeal. You can add layers of complexity by dressing the veggies or greens with a simple dressing based on the leftover Hogan's Marinade. It's pretty simple to separate a yolk from its egg and put it, along with a cup of mari-nade, in a straight-sided cup or jar. If you have a stick blender, use it to whip the mixture. The egg will act as an emulsifier, uniting the oil and the rum into a dressing that won't separate.

You can cheat a bit and use commercial mayonnaise—perhaps two tablespoons in lieu of the egg.

As a Seasoning in Soup or Stew

The dishes that benefit from this are hearty, thickly textured, or strongly flavored. For a soup, you can use Hogan's Marinade in proportions up to about one to ten. That is, for every ten ounces of soup, try an ounce of marinade.

For a stew:

- let the marinade stand until a layer of oil has separated and risen to the top of the container. Pour a few tablespoons of oil into the hot pan.
- brown some beef, pork, or lamb cubes that you've coated in flour, salt, and pepper and transfer to a slow-cooker.
- brown a chopped up onion and some pieces of potato or carrot, adding more oil if necessary. Put them in the slow cooker and add some celery and a handful of fresh chopped herb.
- pour the reserved Hogan's Marinade over the food, cover, and cook on High until desired tenderness is achieved.

You can make a fishy variation on this by browning and slow cooking everything but the meat. When the starchy vegetables are soft, put some chunks of salmon that you've seared in a bowl and cover with the expanded Marinade.

Fish

Rum Cedar-Planked Salmon

Be sure to use cedar that hasn't been treated with chemicals. It's best to inquire carefully at the lumber yard, buy directly from a mill, or spend the extra money on cedar planks at the kitchen supply store.

You can scale this recipe, but it's especially appealing if you present an entire side of salmon on a single plank. Two details: first, always soak any plank, cedar or otherwise, that you're going to put near fire or the wood will go up in flames. Second, be sure to dilute the rum as instructed or the wood will go up in flames. Finally, don't sit on the grill or you will go up in flames.

Salmon filet, skin-on
Cedar planks soaked in five parts water to one part dark rum.
Seasoning rub
Sugar and salt, equal parts
White pepper
Coriander seed
Chopped rosemary
Moisten with enough lemon juice to make a paste

Preheat the grill to a medium low heat (275°F). Put the fish—with pin bones removed—on the plank and cover the flesh side of the filet(s) with the seasoning rub and refrigerate loosely covered for at least half an hour. Cook until the fish is slightly firm to the touch.

The same recipe can be prepared in a smoker, adding the rum to the seasoning rub and adjusting the time accordingly.

Rum-Cured Salmon

If all that smoke and flame is a little too much for your one-bedroom apartment, you can get an elegant appetizer with the same palate of flavor.

Place the salmon filet—again with pin bones removed—on a dish. Make up enough of the same rub to cover the fish and smear it on. Cover with plastic wrap and then add another plate and a pound or more of weight (a half gallon jug filled with water or milk is just right).

In 12 to 30 hours, scrape off the rub and slice the fish thinly on the diagonal. Sprinkle the slices with capers and chopped hard-boiled egg, and graciously accept ooohs and aaahs from your guests.

Rum at the Barbecue

There's a master recipe here and it goes something like this: you marinate meat in a mixture of rum, spices, sugar, salt, and acid. Remove the meat, pat it dry, and grill it. While the meat is improving itself on the grill, boil the marinade until its volume is reduced by half. Spread the thickened marinade (now a sauce) on the meat and serve. Here's an example, but I'm sure you can come up with more.

½ cup (100 ml) dark rum
2 tablespoons (30 ml) lime or lemon juice
2 tablespoons (30 ml) soy sauce
2 tablespoons (30 g) brown sugar

Kansas City barbecue. Photo by Jeffrey J. Martin.

Not all wings are from Buffalo. Photo by Flickr user Taz.

4 cloves garlic, minced

1 small jalapeno pepper, seeded and chopped

1 tablespoon (30 ml) grated ginger

1 teaspoon black pepper

3 boneless chicken breasts, halved

Combine rum, lime juice, soy sauce, sugar, garlic, chilies, ginger, and black pepper. Place chicken in resealable food storage bag; pour marinade over chicken. Press air out of bag and seal tightly. Turn bag over to completely coat chicken with marinade. Refrigerate at least 4 hours.

Drain chicken; reserve the marinade. Grill chicken, in skillet or on uncovered grill, until chicken is firm to the touch and no longer pink. While chicken is cooking, boil marinade until it's reduced by half. Pour the reduced marinade (now a sauce) over the chicken.

Sweet Dishes

The caramel flavor of dark rum makes it a perfect companion to many desserts. Here's a recipe for one of the simplest and most elegant:

Sweet Rum Sauce

Here's a general purpose dessert sauce that enables you to link the flavors of the rum palate to a whole universe of desserts. Quantities are provided, but this scales up to the safe maximum of your pan or down to a spoonful.

2 tablespoons (25 g) butter

2 tablespoons (25 g) white or brown sugar

Tiramisu: rum and coffee-soaked lady fingers with whipped cream and mascarpone in this seductive Italian classic. Photo by Sebastian Kügler.

8 ounces (225 ml) cream or half and half

2 ounces (50 ml) rum

½ teaspoon vanilla

Cook the sugar in the butter over medium-high flame until sugar is fragrant.

Add cream, lower heat, and reduce the sauce slightly.

Add rum and vanilla and simmer until reduced by about half.

This recipe can also be used to make a savory sauce. Omit the vanilla at the end and include a half teaspoon of black pepper in the first step. Both the sweet and savory versions should be quite dark.

Rum Sabayon

Jonathan Deutsch, PhD

Drexel University Center for Hospitality and Sport Management

Many sweet dishes like babas au rhum use rum as a flavorful and boozy soak to bracing effect. Artusi himself suggested the addition of rum to the classic marsala or madera, but rum alone is akin to tasting the rum swirled in a warm creamy snifter. You'll never want to return to the traditional.

Serve over tropical fruit and genoise. Or just about anything else.

Serves 4

4 egg yolks
Zest of half a lime

Sabayon. Photo by Stu Spivack.

One squeeze fresh lime juice

1–1 ½ ounce shot rum

⅓ cup sugar

Splash water

Combine all ingredients in a medium stainless steel bowl or the top of a double boiler. Cook over simmering water, whisking constantly, until it thickens to the texture of melted ice cream. If you get scrambled eggs you've become too hot and gone too far. Start over. You'll get it the second time. Adjust lime juice and sugar to taste.

Rum Custard

Jon Deutsch's Sabayon (Zabaglione) above is probably the king of all dessert sauces. If you're at all intimidated by the "whisk over hot water don't let it curdle" part, here's a universal rum custard recipe.

The usual proportions for a sweet custard are one egg and two tablespoons of sugar for each cup (225 ml) of milk. You can also use half and half or even light cream for a richer custard. An egg to a cup of liquid is the minimum proportion of eggs to milk which will produce properly thickened custard. You may, though, use as many as four eggs and increase the sugar to four tablespoons. Increasing the sugar will make the custard less firm and lengthen the cooking time. Increasing the egg will make the custard firmer and shorten the cooking time.

When you play with this recipe, if you feel you're not getting enough fat, you can also substitute two egg yolks for one whole egg.

3 cups (675 ml) milk or half and half
4 eggs
½ cup (100 g) sugar
1 to 3 tablespoons dark rum (15–45 ml)
½ teaspoon salt (3–4g)
Additional flavoring: nutmeg, cinnamon, allspice

Preheat oven to 350°F/175°C.
Mix milk and well-beaten eggs with sugar, rum, and salt.

Place six to eight baking cups in a pan large enough to hold the cups without them touching the side of the pan or each other. Pour mixture into the cups, sprinkle with ground spice.

Put the pan in the oven and pour very hot water to almost the top of the baking cups. Bake until a knife inserted in the center of the custard comes out clean, maybe 25 to 30 minutes. Remove cups from water bath and cool for 15 minutes. You can cool these custards and top them with fruit or whipped cream, but they will never taste better than they do while they are still just slightly warm.

By the way, if you find yourself enchanted by any of the rum cocktails in chapter 7, you can nudge the flavor of the custard in that direction. Mojito custard? Just crush some mint and lime peel in rum and let it sit for half an hour before you add it in. If you like the combination of coffee and rum, use about ¾ cup (80 g) of whole coffee beans and pour your milk/cream mixture (about a cup and a half—300 g) over it. Allow the mixture to infuse overnight in the refrigerator and then proceed with your custard recipe. Dark roast coffee works best.

A few enthusiasts insist on molasses as a baking ingredient. Photo by Gaetan Lee.

CHAPTER 7

RUM
AND THE
NEW
ALCHEMY

Cocktails

There are an infinite number of possible combinations of ingredients and so much variation in individual tastes that rating cocktails is not just impossible, it's fundamentally wrongheaded.

We'll use this section to look at some of the principles that bring those ingredients together and suggest a few experiments to expand your appreciation of both the purists' and the modernists' approaches.

A note on Alchemy and its casual use in the world of cocktails:

Alchemy is an ancient tradition in the Western and Arabic worlds. In spite of what your chemistry teacher told you, it was never a science, a pseudo-science, or a proto-science. It instead was a spiritual matter: the pursuit of purification and transformation. Alchemy and alchemists represented the ambition of reaching to perfection. The alchemists wondered about the

possibility of perfecting matter (gold was the standard of perfection), perfecting man (becoming immortal), and perfecting the spirit (enlightenment). In many ways, alchemy competed with religion and often its practitioners spoke in a code of their own to avoid conflicts with religious authority. (Such conflicts, you may recall, could have, and still do have, serious consequences for the person on the wrong side of religion. Dante, for instance, places the alchemists in hell, condemned for even trying to change an order that he thought was divinely ordained.)

The modern Western analog to alchemy is probably psychotherapy, maybe it's the self-help movement. The Buddhist analog may be meditation and kindness. These are pretty heavy-duty concerns and they seem pretty far afield from the cocktail bar. So why talk about alchemy here? Why is there a bar called the Alchemist and Barrister? Why do 47.2 percent of articles

Cocktails get sexy during prohibition.

about bartenders call them "alchemists"? (Second only to the 78.1 percent that use the term "mixologist.")

Part of the reason is simply based on tools. Much of the apparatus with which the alchemists conducted their physical experiments is still being used in labs today: many of them have analogs in the bar, distillery, or brew house. Distillation itself is rooted in this tradition and in notions of purification and etherialization of the coarse into the refined.

A firmer connection lies in the very art of the cocktail itself. The bartender takes the given and transforms it into the desired. The ideal cocktail isn't a mere sum of its parts, something to be analyzed and described by tongue and nose. Rum can blend into the background for those drinks that are a bit ashamed of their alcohol or push its way to the front of the crowd and give everyone its boozy blessing. The ideal cocktail is perfectly new,

Photo by Flickr user star5112.

untraceable, unparented. It comes into the world magically, if not divinely. That the alcohol in cocktails works a transformation on the drinker only extends the power of the metaphor. If the transformation is not always towards a higher, better, and purer thing, well, we still haven't made lead into gold yet either.

Tucked inside of every consideration of alcohol is a notion of purity.

* Nothing but grapes in our wine,
* Bavarian Beer "Purity" Law,
* distilled from Nothing But.

Well, listen up, Nothing But, it's time to learn what chefs have known for years. The Art of Delight is an Art—as in *artificium*—to make art, we seek the beautiful which is not necessarily the same as the pure.

We're in the delight business here and if I told you that there was a delightful potion to be made from sugarcane, vanilla bean, and nutmeg and that it had been made for centuries on the island of Goaway, you'd accept that as a serious beverage.

No matter: we are no longer in the land of the Purist. The cocktail chapter is the place where the modernist meets the hedonist: nothing is sacred but delight. I wonder what we can learn from a handful of recipes.

Cocktail Culture

A simple but often unspoken fact is that most of us don't take naturally to the taste of distilled spirits. You've got to want it before you can like it. For confirmation, watch the face of an

HERMETIS
TRISMEGISTI
PHOENICUM ÆGYPTIORUM
Sed et aliarum Gentium
MONARCHÆ CONDITORIS

five
TABULA SMARAGDINA
à fitu temerarÿfq́
nunc demum priftino Genio
Vindicata per
WILHELMUM CHRISTOPHORUM
KRIEGSMANNUM.

DEUTER: XXXIII. vers: 13.14.16.
Benedictum eft à DOMINO terzæ ejus pretiofo
Coeli fructu, Rore; et ex abyffo cubante infer
ne: pretiofo fructu proventuum Solis; et
pretiofo fructu influentiæ Lunæ: pre
tiofo denig'fructu terræ, uberta
tea ejus.
Adjectum eft
Teftamentum Arnoldi de Villa Nova

The first cocktail manual? The *Theosophie Alchemie* dates to at least the eighth century. This is from a seventeenth-century edition known as *The Emerald Tablet*. It contains this direction, which could be considered a call for distillation: "Separate thou the earth from the fire, the subtle from the gross sweetly with great industry."

eight year old as he or she takes a sniff of Daddy's snifter. For young men, there is sometimes a rite of passage that involves taming the childish gullet to accept a burning shot of booze while the already initiated chuckle at his discomfort. Most women, lacking the peer pressure of that rite, never really acquire the yearn for the burn. So for many of us, the taste and feel of alcoholic drinks is a barrier to enjoying alcohol. It's a measure of the delight we take in its effects (See: What Does Alcohol Mean) that we go to some trouble to make it palatable.

We have been at this business of disguising the taste of spirits almost since their invention. Sometimes the disguise is merely categorical, as when we call a shot of booze "bitters" or "medicine" or "tonic." More recently, we soften the taste of booze with sugar and then with fruits and other flavors. Another hidden virtue of the cocktail is that most of them lower the percentage of alcohol in your glass. The less-alcoholic drink stretches the evening out, making a social beverage into a more sociable one.

So let us consider cocktails. Since it's almost impossible to "spoil" them, there are an infinite possible number of recipes and—especially in the case of rum—you could generate thousands of cocktails with a Random Rum Cocktail Generator. The basic algorithm for the RRCG would be something like this:

- take a volume of some sort of rum
- add two volumes of a fruit juice
- include a small amount of sweetener
- add a small amount of sour (lemon, lime and pineapple are examples)
- pick a spice or herb and dust it in lightly

Flourishes might include:

- a bit of bitter
- a splash of soda, flavored or plain

A good way to consider the possible variations is to imagine that each recipe has a central ingredient or that it embodies a tension between two ingredients. With that in mind, you can read a cocktail recipe as a depiction of a theme. If you understand the theme, you can then run a gazillion variations from it.

This is the organizing principle behind this chapter. Let's entertain some themes, some of them obvious and others surprising. Once we have our themes, you can spin the ingredient wheel and decide which variations to pursue. As a fertile fr'instance, let's consider The Silkman. (This, and all the other recipes are reprinted just as I got them from the sources.)

The Silkman

From the Mississippi Gulf Coast, here's the house cocktail of Tim and Brenda Silkman. This is a pretty high-impact drink that shows off best in an old fashion glass. Tim Silkman explains:

"This has been a go-to drink since the first time I made it. Not too sweet and good and rummy, a drink that makes you want another. Which I do!"

1 ½ ounces Appleton Jamaican Rum-Special
¾ ounces Bacardi 151
1 ½ ounces orange juice (fresh squeezed if ya got it)
1 tablespoon cherry juice

1 quarter wedge of lime (toss in drink)
1 or 2 shakes of Angostura bitters

You can find frozen cherry juice from time to time, but it's easier to buy, defrost, and puree frozen cherries. In some parts of the country, cherry growers press excess cherries into juice. (If you can resist the temptation to ferment it into cider or put it in your homebrewed Belgian-style beer, you might freeze little cubes of it and play with it later in Cocktailland). The Silkmans put their mix in a pint mason jar (good southern cocktail shaker) with cracked ice and give it a few good shakes. They pour it over a few whole ice cubes (strain the cracked ice) pop in a whole cherry and enjoy.

So what's going on here? The basic waltz is between orange and cherry juice: sweet-tart and earthy-tart.

Once you have that, you can add rum:

How does the rum act in the middle of that tension? This rum has aromas of caramel, spices, toasted wood. The fruit tastes ripen and mature in their presence. The finish gives off the scent of caramel, toffee, and there are hints of ripe banana and brown sugar. This is, if you'll allow all those flavors in the rum, a knitting together of sweetness and tartness with a chord of flavors that are examples of both. Caramel and toffee? Sugar's naughty descendants. Banana? Brown sugar? Flavors standing right at the intersection of sweet-earth and tart, both of them waiting to make peace or get run over in the process.

So now you have a grand harmony, and too much harmony in novels and cocktails, as you know, is boring. So what do we do to spice things up? How can we start a ruckus, if not a fight?

- bitter it up with Angostura
- fizz it out with soda or sparkling wine
- increase the tartness with lemon or more lime
- sweeten it with more sugar or honey or cane juice
- garnish with mint or a strip of orange peel

Try it with different types of rums for a completely different drink and back off on the 151 for a gentler, almost wine-like beverage. Remember that the cracked ice in the cocktail shaker (or Mason jar or vacant goldfish bowl) dilutes the 151 and lowers its proof.

You get the idea. If cocktail recipes are about a central tension, a drama-like play of one ingredient off another, then really a cocktail recipe collection should give you the main characters (cherry/orange/rum in this case) and then perhaps a few suggestions for the supporting cast with the understanding that you can—and should—try a bunch of different possibilities.

So here's a bunch of rum cocktails. Each recipe has two or three starring ingredients. Sometimes the rum is a star, sometimes not. You could take any one of them and use it as the theme of cocktails for the rest of your life. Or you could take three or four of your favorites and never run the risk of boring anybody—including yourself.

The role of the rum itself is highly variable. In general, the browner the rum, the more forward it's going to be and the more the other ingredient have to harmonize with it. Lighter rums tend to be more diffident, hiding behind the more pungent ingredients and adding just their heat.

So here are some major themes—some high dramas and low comedies—that are compatible with rum. Try them all, keep a few, share with your friends—let me know.

The Mojito

Many people of a certain generation consider this drink to be the reason that rum was invented. Let's look at the procedure:

Place ten mint leaves and one lime wedge into a sturdy glass. Consider the aromas: imagine the fragrance of those ten mint leaves as you pluck them from the stem and drop them in the glass. This may be one of the few times that mint ever presents itself as a subtlety—its aroma oily and elusive. Then the lime, juice and peel both sweet, both sharp and candy-like. The sturdy glass in your hand—a tumbler or an old fashioned glass perhaps—is as solid and weighted to the earth as your ingredients are airy and high-flying.

Use a muddler to crush leaves of mint and lime to release the mint oils and lime juice. Now you've done it! Your hands smell, the glass smells, and it's all rising up from the counter. These two unsubtle ingredients are bruised in the bottom of the glass, but their aromas are blended and floating it the air around you.

Add two more lime wedges and some sugar, and muddle again to release the lime juice. The rubbery lime peels are stubbornly resisting, in fact mocking your attempt to make a drink out of them. The more you muddle, the more of a muddle you're in. The drink becomes more fragrant and more undrinkable as you work it. The grit of the sugar—before it

Photo by Flickr user Paul Gy.

dissolves—is the antithesis of drinkability. (Professional bartenders keep some already-dissolved sugar in the form of simple syrup on hand.)

Fill the glass almost to the top with ice. Hah! Take that you pushy aromatics! We've physically buried all those oily boys and reduced their volatility at the same time. The glass, which had been warm from your effort, is beginning to chill in your hand.

Pour one and a half ounces of white or gold rum (40 ml) over the ice. You're making a tincture, you know: extracting the flavor of mint and lime into the alcohol of the rum where they are happy to live and be preserved. For a minute, you have a brand-new liquor in front of you. We'll call it Canelimuhmint. But wait: you've made a new ingredient, dense and adhesive. What you wanted was a drink, filled with liquid and light.

So you fill the glass with carbonated water. All the tension that was locked, dense and brooding in the glass is released. Little bubbles of carbon dioxide carry the story to your nose, the liquid turns the dense drama into gliding liquid taste.

Garnish with the remaining lime wedge. Ach, we almost forgot to include a little treat for the eye, a small announcement that this wasn't pedestrian soda pop. You can squeeze the lime, drop it in the glass and thereby become a co-creator of the transformation.

This one is from Amada, the flagship of the Jose Garces restaurant group. The organization is noted for exciting restaurant environments, good food, and a savvy attention to their drinks list.

"Our menu currently features a cocktail that we like to call *I'm So Excited* named after the Pedro Almodóvar film. (All of our specialty cocktails are named after his films.)" The ingredients for this drink are as follows:

1 ounce cantaloupe puree
1 ½ ounce white rum
½ ounce mint and red pepper simple syrup
½ ounce lime juice

Combine all ingredients over ice, shake, and pour in Collins/highball glass. Garnish with fresh mint leaf.

A very delicious and refreshing cocktail with a little kick!

You may recognize the theme from the Silkman cocktail: rum and fruit and sweet and sour. This time the fruit is puréed fresh cantaloupe, a light-bodied melon that's wonderfully aromatic when it's ripe. It's a theme that's ready for expansion. Any peeled, ripe, puréed fruit can be substituted for the cantaloupe and you can nudge the flavor of simple syrup any way you want.

A drink like this is a perfect place to show off the season's produce at its best, but if the calendar is against you, chunks of defrosted frozen fruit can be puréed in a blender (isn't that why they have "purée" settings?).

Note that there is a bit of equipment involved here. The cantaloupe doesn't puree itself, so you need an electric blender. In the days before Fred Waring created the first one, you could use a food mill to puree a fruit, but most of us were unlikely to do that particularly tedious job. The electric blender made fruit purée available to those of us without hired help. Not incidentally, the blender is a transformative tool in itself, the solid becomes liquid: what had to be chewed can now be drunk.

> There is a recipe in the cancer comedy book *Radiation Days* for a blender drink that makes it possible for a sick or weak person to get nourished. We'll call that drink the Life Saver.

Of course, these new semi-liquid fruits can all become the bases for a whole new generation of drinks. Today, you can tell if your bar is even slightly modernist by the presence of a blender on the back bar.

Piña Colada

This drink is a screen, a luscious fruity way to make believe that there's no alcohol involved and we're all just sitting around celebrating tropical fruits and our common Caribbean heritage. It's one of the few popular rum drinks that's sometimes served without rum. The rumless version is called a "virgin" Piña Colada and the coinage tells you a lot about the mythic place of booze in the Western World.

The drink dates back at least to the early fifties and certainly to Puerto Rico. Authorship is claimed by the Barrachina Restaurant, 104 Fortaleza Street, Old San Juan and the Beachcomber Bar at the luxury flagship Caribe Hilton popularized it. The Caribe Hilton popularized San Juan as a tourist destination, so maybe we should believe them.

Consider one version of the drink:

In a cocktail shaker, pour two ounces of pineapple juice and two ounces (50 ml) of Coco Lopez coconut cream. Coconut cream is essentially a water extract of shredded coconut (coconut milk) that's been cooked and concentrated. It's a thick and fatty essence of coconut, a mouth-coating balm. Fresh pineapple juice has an enzyme called bromelain that attacks the protein in your mouth (it's occasionally used as a meat tenderizer). The two fight it out: prickly and smooth and the aromas that rise above the battle are pure essence of tropic.

Add ice and 1 ½ (40 ml) ounces of white rum. White rum is pretty mild stuff, noticeable mostly for the burn of alcohol. Underneath all the drama and clamor of coconut fat and attack pineapple, will you notice the burn? Not likely. What we have now is a stealth alcohol delivery system: fifteen to twenty grams of alcohol disguised as something that tastes like ice cream.

Photo by Randy Robertson.

Add one ounce (25 ml) dark rum Okay, a little truth in advertising here, the dark rum will poke through to announce that this is in fact an alcoholic drink, but the dark rum also has its own sugary, molasses cloak to hide behind.

Shake, strain, and pour into a martini glass A martini glass? Are we now feeling all sophisticated and grown up with a drink that's composed of childhood and childish favorite tastes?

Note that we usually detect the presence of alcohol by a burning sensation that results from alcohol's hygroscopic (water stealing) propensities. The addition of the coconut cream hides the burn and makes this drink deceptively childlike.

Puerto Rico has a National Piña Colada day on July 10. What should we do to celebrate?

Planter's Punch

What a name! It suggests a life of linen-suited ease on a breezy veranda, a kind of chummy privilege. It's a name that's used throughout the Caribbean in tourist-oriented bars. Everyplace else in the islands, we ask for the simpler "rum punch." And ask for it we do. There is hardly a restaurant, bar, or friendly household that doesn't have a recipe for punch.

The idea of punch comes into the English-speaking world from India. (The word comes from the Sanskrit *panc* meaning five, as the original had five ingredients: alcohol, sugar, lemon, water, and spice). The idea is to make a sweet, lower-alcohol drink that's cheap to concoct and that makes the party last a little bit longer.

Here's a recipe verbatim from the now-defunct www.st croix-beaches.com.

RUM PUNCH: This popular rum drink is quite often served complimentary at events. Quick and easy. Definitely "Party Time" with Caribbean Rum Punch Recipes.

Splash of lemon juice
2 cups Cruzan light rum
2 liters ginger ale
1 qt. fruit punch
1 qt. orange juice or pineapple juice
Ice cubes

Pour into punch bowl. Stir well. To serve: pour over one ice cube in each glass.

There are a few things worth noting:

"This popular rum drink is quite often served complimentary at events."

That's another way of saying that it's cheap to make and the rum is diluted down with sugar water to a point that reduces the chance of mass drunkenness. In St. Croix at least, Cruzan rum is not taxed and is less expensive than soda pop.

"1 qt. fruit punch"

Where do you find fruit punch? On a tree? No, it's in a can at the supermarket alongside the pineapple and lemon juice—this is a quick and dirty, can-openers' recipe.

"lice cubes"

Typos aside, the drink is going to be cold so the sweetness will be less noticeable and the alcohol will be diluted even more by the ice.

Photo by Flickr user scaredykat.

Fish House Punch

The Original Fish House Punch was a knock-'em-stupid pow-erhouse that disguised its alcohol level behind a veil of sweet-ness. This version is the famous, very potent, traditional house punch of the State in Schuylkill, an exclusive Philadelphia fishing club founded in 1732. ("Exclusive" in this context means White, Anglo-Saxon, and Rich.) It is in many ways the opposite of the Rum Punch above: designed to change the mood of a company in very short order.

The recipe is preserved and occasionally used by the much more egalitarian Philadelphia Canoe and Kayak Club. Their current boathouse was called, from 1876 to 1887, the Colony of the State in Schuylkill, or Colony Castle. The recipe is passed along courtesy of Marion Ambros, who in his capacity as Com-modore has seen a few punch bowls drained.

Two quarts Jamaica rum

One quart brandy

One-half pint peach brandy

One-half pint Maraschino liquor

One quart green tea

One pint fresh lemon juice

One pound of sugar

One bottle Champagne

A quick calculation shows that this punch would have quite a punch. The only dilution is with the green tea so its alcohol by volume should be around 35 percent, or scarcely less than the ABV of the straight rum itself. Make it with a dark rum like Myer's and black tea and without the Maraschino and peach brandies for a surprisingly sophisticated drink.

The Napoleon: Short and Tall/Light or Dark

Courtesy of the Chestnut Grill

The Chestnut Grill is a legendary bar and sidewalk café in one of those tree-lined neighborhoods that makes Philadelphia sometimes seem like a country town. The recipe is courtesy of Greg Welsh, owner and chief storyteller. As an amateur historian, he claims to be amused by the notion of a Tall Napoleon. This variation on the basic rum cocktail uses a liqueur—essentially a concentrated fruit flavor bomb, a pourable Jolly Rancher—as fortification for the fruit juice.

Welsh writes:

Your Basic (short) Napoleon:

> 1 ½ ounces of rum
> 1 ½ ounces of Joseph Cartron Pamplemousse Liqueur
> Pour over ice and stir before serving.

Your Tall Napoleon

> 1 ½ ounces of rum
> 1 ½ ounces of Joseph Cartron Pamplemousse Liqueur
> Pour over ice in a tall glass, top with grapefruit juice
> The tall Napoleon is surprisingly ethereal and refreshing

Light and Dark

The light Napoleon is essentially a fruit drink: grapefruit doubled down with the liqueur.

Made with dark rum, the dark Napoleon extends the fruitiness of the drink in the citric direction, but the impression of a short, concentrated boozy character remains. The addition of soda in the tall version moves us over into a crisp, almost ascetic delight. From Janis Joplin, let's say, to Nina Simone.

Now the savvy cocktail alchemist will probably extend this formula. Orange curaçao, rum, and orange juice? Of course. Cherry Heering, crushed cherries, and rum? Excellent. For about a month in the summer, you might consider Chambord, rum, and crushed black raspberries (see "I'm So Excited.")

Of course, from the inclusion of fruit liqueurs in your cocktails, it's just a short step to using rum to make a liqueur of your own. For instance:

Take one pound of perfectly ripe peaches. Cut away any bruises and then cut the fruit into small pieces. Place the chopped peach in a non-reactive container with 3 cups (700 ml) of white or amber rum. Cover and store in the proverbial cool, dark place for two or three weeks. Strain the fruit-flavored rum into another container and add a cup (250 ml) of granulated sugar. The rum soaked fruit can be sweetened and used as a topping on crepes or ice cream. Some people would simply eat it with a spoon and grin.

Allow the flavored rum to mature for a month or so, tasting regularly to assure quality control. You may find that your liqueur is quite delightful by itself or you may add it back to fruit juice drinks. It's common for homemade cordials to lose apparent sweetness as they age (mine always do). If you find that to be so, you can adjust the sweetness of yours by simply adding more sugar. If you overcorrect, try adding a bit more rum.

The inclusion of more than one distilled spirit in a drink serves to remind us that two liquors together don't necessarily cancel each other out. The result can sometimes be a harmony. Purists, of course, are aghast but the modernists rejoice. Here's an example from Philadelphia banker Jim Shrader:

> For a really fun night Diane and I like to get . . .
> . . . between the sheets
> Equal parts cognac, aged rum and Grand Marnier
> Fresh lemon juice to taste
> Shake and pour into a martini glass

The cognac and the rum are both wood-aged. One refers back to wine, the other to cane. The Grand Marnier is sweet and citrusy. To get enough orange to intrude on the rum cognac conversation, you necessarily end up with a drink that's cloyingly sweet, so the lemon "corrects" to a better balance and adds its own citrus flavor.

The Cool Stroker

Is in the spirit of Cherries Jubilee, a drink with lots of visual appeal that's fun long before you taste it. Drinks like this are often the specialty of bars which are likely to stock exotic ingredients. Many of my readers might find themselves low on Sage liqueur, Nocello, and Manä, so it's easier to walk into the bar at the Rittenhouse Hotel and ask Justin for a Cool Stroker. Try not to giggle when you do, the drink itself is very good and sitting in this bar lets you think you're important for an hour or so (for most of us, that's a pretty radical alchemical transformation).

Papi Hurtado is the source of the Cool Stroker and the Master Mixologist at the Rittenhouse Library Bar.

Cool Stroker

> 2 ounces Rum Appleton Estate reserve
> ½ ounce Nocello walnut liqueur
> ¼ ounce Sage liqueur
> 1 ½ ounces Manà *
> ¾ ounces fresh pineapple juice
> 3 little drops vanilla extract
> 5 sage leaves

---

* Manà is made simple: add 1 egg white with the same proportion of Simple syrup. (This is NOT the original "Manà nectar" but is an easy way to make your drink.)

In a cocktail shaker add all the ingredients with ice and shake it don't fake it. Single strain into a cocktail glass (martini) and garnish with a sage leaf.

Before you strain the cocktail into the martini glass, light a sage leaf and just burn the leaf and allow the smoke to get into the glass. The leaf will float on the drink, daring you to figure out just where to put your lips. In my experience, questions like that can be the start of some very interesting conversations.

Rum and Coffee, Coffee and Rum

A shot of rum in a cup of hot coffee or a glass of iced coffee seems like a pretty obvious move. Coffee and sugar are old friends: many coffee lovers can only consummate their relationship with the black stuff by adding a bit of sugar. Of course, there's a natural antagonism too. As anthropologist Leon Stover was wont to observe, coffee and alcohol drinks "build you up while they tear you down." So, while encouraging moderation in this as in all things, let me urge you to explore this marriage made in the tropics.

But beware: when rum (which, after all, is sugar's first cousin) meets coffee, something odd happens. Even a small volume of rum tends to overwhelm the coffee's flavor and aroma. In hot coffee, the effect is especially perverse—the heat of the coffee vaporizes the alcohol in the rum and what started out as a roasty-toasty embrace of coffee turns into something that's more like huffing pure alcohol fumes. In iced coffee, the fumy presence is less of a problem, but the boozy bite of the rum seriously diminishes the coffee's aroma and body.

What to do? There are two solutions and they are both elegant in their own way. The first is simply to infuse a portion of

Flaming rum extinguished with coffee liqueur and strong sweet coffee. Photo by Flickr user Miquel C.

rum with finely-ground coffee, let it sit overnight and then filter the rum. After extensive laboratory testing, we here at the Short Course in Rum can't find much difference between filter drip processing and French Press.

Here's a typical recipe:
2 ounces coffee (50 g), coarsely ground
6 ounces (150 ml) 80 proof rum

Combine in a covered jar and allow to macerate overnight. Pour off the rum, allow it to settle and pour off again if necessary.

A modern copper still at the La Colombe distillery and coffee house.

The second is to find a rum that's been blended with coffee. Why pay someone else to do the work for you? Because extraction's a risky business, or at least a crafty one. The flavors that you and I extract in our kitchens are only a part of what coffee has to offer. The best possible job is done under conditions that are far more controlled than we can achieve. Right now, the best possible coffee-rum marriage is being celebrated in A Different Drum. ADD, as we like to call it, is made by a coffee roaster who is also a rum producer. La Colombe coffee is one of America's premier roasters—it exports coffee to the rest of the world.

Finally, rum is an ingredient in lots of home remedies.

Medicine for a Sore Throat—Puerto Rico

This mixture was recommended by a chiropractor who was born in Puerto Rico. Note the specificity of the upper class Bacardi Rum rather than the more commonly available Don Q.

6 ounces Bacardi

4 ounces honey

2 squeezed lemons

⅛ teaspoon granulated (candied) ginger

⅛ teaspoon ground cinnamon

Mix thoroughly in a clear jar and leave in a sunny place for a week.

Strain, add 6 ounces Bacardi, and refrigerate.

Take one tablespoon swallowed slowly for a sore throat.

CHAPTER 8

FURTHER RUM READING (AND TRAVEL)

**"I drink because drinking makes it less
lonely in here."**

—*Emanuel Cardoso*

There is something perverse going on here.

If you tell people that you're writing a book about a drink, beer let's say or even rum, the response is almost always a smile. There's something inherently frivolous about an interest in alcohol, people entertain the suspicion that your "scholarship" is really just a veil over some darker interest or evidence of a lack of the ability to deal with more serious things.

And yet, as I look over the list of books that I consulted as I put this one together, I'm struck by how much top-quality writing and/or scholarship I found. There's the breezy insouciance of Ian Williams for instance and here's the thoughtful sophistication of Charles William Taussig. (The same could be said of beer. Michael Jackson, Randy Mosher, and Bill Bryson are all sophisticated voices drawn to an ostensibly plebian or at best frivolous subject.)

There's "serious" scholarship here too. In spite of occasionally ponderous prose, Sidney Mintz's *Sweetness and Power* is a challenging milestone in looking at how the tiny levers of consumption sometimes move the supposedly larger worlds of politics and power. Charlotte Sussman rather cleverly cut to the core in *Women and the Politics of Sugar*.

Drinking itself and inebriation blissful or demonic have attracted their share of thoughtful and elegant writers. The *New York Times* itself has assembled an all-star team for the online anthological blog "Proof: Alcohol and American Life."

So what's goin' on here?

Part of the answer is obvious: Many writers drink and find the writing to be better for it. Many drinkers write and don't have far to look for a subject. To go a step further: most of those writing drinkers and almost all of those drinking writers are also readers. To read good drinking writing, I'm told, is almost as much fun as drinking, so there's an audience there.

But I suspect that there's more here than the simple matter of readers taking in each other's wash.

Then there's the question of stage fright and self-doubt. Writers rarely see their audiences but are no less afraid of them, and almost everything that can be said about alcohol and courage has been.

Lurking in the background is also the difficult and undeniable fact that drinking and poetry have been connected for as long as they both have existed.

"Wine's the train the Muse takes into town."
—Joan Adler

How does that work? How do inebriation and inspiration find each other? How do they do it so frequently? It's a question that terrifies prohibitionists and writers alike. If in wine there is beauty (as well as truth) then what's the point of railing against wine? And what sort of person would want to? On the other hand, if all of Dylan Thomas is 32 percent whiskey and 68 percent Thomas, isn't the writer's self-esteem and sense of accomplishment on pretty shaky conceptual ground here?

Of course, I raise these questions not to answer them, but simply to call for more. More reading, more writing, and yes, more drinking. Here are a few items that may be worthy of your consideration.

YO-HO-HO AND A BOTTLE OF RUM.

Rum has a legitimate historical connection with piracy and the Caribbean and this little verse isn't part of it. It was written by Robert Louis Stevenson and published in his 1883 novel *Treasure Island*. Stevenson only gave us the title and a fragment.

Fifteen men on a dead man's chest—
Yo ho ho! And a bottle of rum!
Drink and the devil had done for the rest—
Yo ho ho and a bottle of rum.

In spite of this thin-bodied spirit of an origin, the song has been fleshed out and reused in several movie versions of *Treasure Island* and even as background music for an amusement park ride at the wholesome Disney World. By the way, the Dead Man's Chest in the title has nothing to do with a dance involving more than two dozen men in a particularly small area. It refers to the custom of auctioning off or raffling the sea chest of a man who died.

Books

Caribbean Rum: A Social and Economic History
The Archaeology of Alcohol and Drinking
by Frederick H. Smith

Caribbean Rum describes the role of rum in the plantation system of the Caribbean since the sixteenth century. Smith is the right man with the right background to place rum in its proper cultural context. This book draws on documentary, archaeological, and ethnographic evidence from Africa, Europe, and the Americas. Contains the best description of the place rum came to have in West African religion and funeral rites. Smith is a solid scholar and a competent writer.

The Archaeology of Alcohol and Drinking is a delight. By focusing on the physical evidence of alcohol's production and use, it's especially valuable as a resource for understanding the shift from home to industrial production of alcohol. Smith is willing to overreach his discipline a bit in allowing that sometimes alcohol is nothing more than a temporary relief from the stresses of everyday living.

Mastery, Tyranny, and Desire: Thomas Thistlewood and His Slaves
in the Anglo-Jamaican World
by Trevor Burnard

Thomas Thistlewood was an Englishman who emigrated to Jamaica in 1758 and for thirty-six years was a planter, a landowner, and an overseer of slaves. His fourteen thousand page diary details the particulars of that life in details that are both achingly mundane and casually horrifying. If you need to be reminded of Hannah Arendt's equation of banality and evil:

here's your book. Details of household management in the tropics are interspersed with casual accounts of brutal sadism and both are related with the same flat affect.

Thistlewood routinely punished his slaves with floggings and other grotesque punishments. One of his preferred punishments was the "Derby's dose" in which a slave would be forced to defecate into another slave's mouth which would then be forced shut for several hours.

If there is anyone left who would romanticize slave-holding either past or present, this book should be both required reading and sufficient antidote. If the reader can contain her stomach, it also offers some documentation of life of master and slave and the political reality that made slavery and sugar possible.

Rum: A Social and Sociable History of the Real Spirit of 1776
by Ian Williams

Williams is a freelance writer who has adhered to scholarly standards to produce a book with a strong point of view. He maintains that the economic and social role of rum in Colonial America has been systematically suppressed by prohibitionist sentiment and prejudice. He is also unremittingly Anglo-centric, a bizarre take on the cultural world of which we get too little here.

The book is rich in primary sources and it's an excellent starting point for discovering more about the world of rum.

The Table Comes First by Adam Gopnik

Gopnik is the smartest guy in the room and this funny, far-ranging book is about a great deal more than drinking. One high point of *The Table Comes First* is the author's account of taking the writers Mordecai Richtler and Wilfred Sheed out for a monthly drunken lunch.

The Trip to Echo Spring by Olivia Lang

This is an engaging but gloomy book written by a Brit who seems to be more fascinated with American alcoholic writers than with her boozy countrymen. She talks about the role of alcohol in the life and work of John Berryman, Raymond Carver, John Cheever, F. Scott Fitzgerald, Ernest Hemingway, and Tennessee Williams. She advances the plausible hypothesis that writing and drinking are both attempts to pacify fearsome loneliness. Hemingway's observation that he drank "to make other people more interesting" isn't far from Lang's idea.

The Distillers Guide to Rum by Ian Smiley, Eric Watson and Michael Delevante

Not for the general reader, this book is intended for the person who knows enough about distillation production to at least have fantasized about that fabulous batch of rum or bourbon that they'll make one day. You would at least have to have brewed a batch of homemade beer to get the most out of it.

The illustrated chapters on the distillation process are the best, and his description of considerations for fermenting the wash are invaluable. You could easily use them and the fermentation recipes provided to produce a batch of rum ready for aging.

The Wet and the Dry: A Drinker's Journey by Lawrence Osborne

Osborne is the author of the novel, *The Forgiven*. He's also an adventurer, travel writer, and author of the wonderfully voyeuristic *Bangkok Days* and one of the funniest wine books ever: *The Accidental Connoisseur*. This is the story of travels in Muslim countries in search of a drink—a trip which offers him a leisurely meditation on drinks and drinking

It's safe to say that his relationship with alcohol is both intimate and conflicted. He writes "The reasons for hating (alcohol) are all valid. But by the same token, they are not reasons at all. For in the end, alcohol is merely us, a materialization of our own natures."

The Fine Art of Mixing Drinks by David A. Embury

Embury was a lawyer and a wit. He must have been a delight to drink with and this book, published in 1948, is a milestone in substance as well as style. *The Fine Art* is notable in its organization of cocktails into two main types: aromatic and sour. Embury categorized ingredients into three categories: "the base, modifying agents, and special flavorings and coloring agents."

He also laid down what should be an eternal rule for all adult beverages. They should whet the appetite rather than stanch it. So an anathema on sweets, creams, and eggs. His emphasis on lots of ice firmly places him in the modernist camp.

An interesting historical artifact: Embury urges the use of large cocktail glasses—at least 3 ounces! This was a man who survived (and presumably defied) Prohibition. If you have even a trace of the bibliophile in you, try to find the 1948 edition.

Proof: The Science of Booze by Adam Rodgers

This is the book that should be packaged with this one. Rodgers claims to be writing about the science of booze, but he's also writing the history, culture, lore, and romance of the stuff. If books like *Short Course in Rum* try to drill down into the depths of a particular spirit, Rodgers tries to lead you up to the mountain for the grand view from horizon to horizon.

The fact that he is both erudite and a graceful writer makes this book an entertainment as well as a delight.

The Buccaneers of America by Alexander Exquemelin

This is the authoritative first-person account of the life and exploits of the maritime outlaws who became known as Buccaneers. It was published in the Netherlands in 1678 as *De Americanensche Zeerovers*. Particularly enlightening is the story of Henry Morgan, whose namesake is a popular modern rum. Exquemelin knew Morgan and presumably interviewed him. The book damaged Morgan's reputation (he lived until 1688) and he successfully sued the publishers.

This is not only first-rate reading but it is an early example of maritime history that belongs on every frustrated sailor's bookshelf.

Websites

The Ministry of Rum: www.ministryofrum.com

The Ministry is an ambitious, humane, and well-constructed website. It has become, over the years, a source for information about rum producers and a conduit for them to reach a public. The artisan distillery movement would have had to invent the

Ministry if Edward Hamilton hadn't. Be sure to check out the interviews in which a curious Hamilton visits various distillers and tastes the rum on camera: the video of him at Zacapa, tasting Ron Zacapa Centenario gives you an idea of how complex and interesting rum can be.

Rum Travel

Anyone who has lived in the Caribbean will be quick to tell you that there are almost as many worlds as there are islands. The British Virgin Islands are a world apart from their American neighbors. Dutch and French islands are closer in some ways to their home countries than to each other. Haiti and the Dominican Republic share a border but not much else.

Among the few slender threads that tie the whole region together, rum is conspicuous. Sugar is now the footnote to the story of the exotic, expanding world of rum. Even islands like St. Croix that no longer raise cane continue to make rum. Some islands in which cane didn't thrive—St. Eustatius and Curaçao for instance—had good harbors and active trading and so enjoy a centuries-old relationship with rum.

So frankly, all Caribbean tourism is rum tourism. You can barely dine without it. If you are looking for history and culture, they overlap everywhere with rum. Even if you want nothing more than a soul-restoring trop-flop, there's a good chance that rum will raise its sugary head.

Tourism officials in the Caribbean are well aware of the power of rum as a tourist draw. Although the islands have been largely off the gourmet travelers' list, rum tours are developing. Check the tourist offices of any of the major rum-producing

Barbados is learning the value of its rum heritage. This is the last wind-powered sugar mill on the island. Photo by Postdlf.

islands for the availability of tasting tours. By all means, consult your favorite distillery, many of them are awake to the possibility of earning customer loyalty through creative hospitality.

The company was originally owned by a man named John Sober. Tours of the distillery and tasting room are now a major attraction for Barbados. Photo by Captmundo.

The webpage for Cruzan Rum (www.cruzanrum.com) plays on the merging of the rum with the island and its slow-paced way of life.

Rum is made in places like this. Photo by Jason P. Heym/Seascape Pool Center Inc.

Not places like this.

CHAPTER 9
THE SHORT COURSE IN RUM TASTING (SCIRT) KIT

Describing the taste of rum is inherently difficult; lots of individual sensations come at you at once. It seems that the best rums are tapestries of a handful of flavors woven together and it's hard to untangle all the threads. The mission of the SCIRT kit is to present one thread at a time.

Wine-tasters have similar kits. You may have seen sets of bottled aromas that break down the taste of wine, whiskey, and coffee into individual sampling jars. There are even tasting kits that let you compare the contribution of different varieties of oak and ones that point to various flaws in wine.

One wine kit from the British outfit, *Le Nez du Vin* costs 120 $US and focuses on wine faults and offers these aromas: Vegetal, Rotten Apple, Vinegar, Glue, Soap, Sulfur, Rotten Egg, Onion, Cauliflower, Horse, Moldy-Earth, and Cork. Kinda makes you thirsty, doesn't it?

Assemble at least six clean small jars with lids, and a bottle of white rum or vodka. For the beginning kit, find these aroma sources:

cinnamon sticks

vanilla bean

almond (extract is good)

prunes

nutmeg

brown sugar

honey

oak chips

light molasses

Each jar gets one of the aroma sources. This mixture of an aromatic substance and alcohol is called a tincture. You'll want to use just enough of each tincture that the aroma is pronounced but not overwhelming. A bit of experimentation will be in order, but you might start with a chopped vanilla bean in one jar and a tablespoon of molasses in another. Then add two ounces of the neutral spirit to each glass jar. Close the jars and put them someplace cool and dark for a few days.

When it's time for the tasting, pour a measure of the rum you want to explore into a glass—a snifter or tulip shaped glass is best. It's probably wisest to start with an aged rum that's intended to be enjoyed by itself. Gather your aroma jars—it's best if they're at the same temperature as your rum. Open one of the bottles—vanilla is a good place to start—and take a small, tentative sniff, holding your nose a few inches away from the open bottle. You want just a hint of the aroma, just enough to make a memory.

Next, swirl the rum in the glass and take a big greedy sniff. Be dramatic, make it a snort. You want to get as much of the aroma in that first sniff as you can. Is there anything of the smell from the jar in the aroma of the rum? Go back a second time to make sure, but take your time between snorts: remember that your sense of smell needs to reset itself: at least thirty seconds.

If you find the smell of vanilla in your target rum, move on. It's a pretty good bet that molasses is in there too.

Continue on (as long as it's fun). You'll certainly find a spice or two and lots of rums have a distinct dried fruit component. You may end up with an impression of three or more distinct aromas on your first try.

If you find that exploring smells this way adds to your pleasure, you can try some other aromas. A useful list for rum might include: caramel, tobacco(!), coconut, toasted coconut, bananas, honey, pineapple fresh or dried, chocolate, orange peel, apple, coffee, coco, dried fruits (raisin, apricot, prunes), sherry, pepper, grass, smoke, toasted sweet potato, and toffee. You can buy some of these already made in the extract section of the spice shop or supermarket, but if you were really into short cuts, you probably wouldn't be doing this in the first place. Of course, you could experience these aromas all by themselves, scrape the chocolate, crack the coconut, but the alcohol preparation makes it easier and—except for the tobacco—you can always use the left-over homemade liquor in cooking or cocktails.

Counterfeit Rum

If you've played with your tasting kit a while, you may want to take the game to the next level. You can use your flavor samples to make your own version of rum. I know that the purists among you are gasping in disbelief, but bear with me, we're going to use this experiment to discover something about our own preferences.

In the Tasting Kit experiment, you may have found that there were some aromas that were particularly beguiling, ones that had your personal email as it were. In the Counterfeit Rum experiment, we're going to build a replica of that rum. We're not going to do that because it's easy, we're going to do it because it's almost impossible but very enlightening.

Let's go back to the aroma jars, this time armed with an eyedropper. Start with a small portion (2 ounces, 50 ml) of vodka or white rum at cool room temperature. Add a few drops of one of the flavors that you found dominant in the first experiment: let's say vanilla or molasses. Smell the result. Add more until the impression is distinct but not overwhelming. Taking time to let your nose recover, move on to other aromas. Be gentle, using single drops. If you're blessed with patience or can counterfeit that virtue for a while, you may find that your counterfeited rum changes as it sits in the glass, the scent of vanilla for instance becoming stronger after a five or ten minute wait. Molasses also seem to become more penetrating after a few minutes time.

When the dominant scents have had a chance to stabilize in the glass, introduce hints of the others. At some point, the drink in your glass is going to smell and taste like rum. What's more startling is that it's very likely that your counterfeit rum will be very good indeed.

As you can imagine, this is a perfect party game. Gather a group and give it a go. Invite people to bring their own flavors. As

CHARTREUSE VEP

The monks who make Chartreuse have decided to join the modernists (although you could make a case that the very idea of modernism in spirits belongs to them): they take a portion of their liqueur and age it in wooden barrels. The VEP stands for Vieillissement Exceptionnellement Prolongé, meaning "exceptionally prolonged aging." Chartreuse VEP comes in both their signature green color and a less pungent but very pretty yellow.

the evening goes on, add ice, wax philosophical, compare yourselves to the alchemists, transform some kind of dross into gold.

At the least, you'll come out of the experience with a heightened sensitivity to the flavor of rum. If you're the sort of person who's inclined to excess, you want to over-flavor the liquid in your glass. Feel free to dissolve a pinch of sugar along with the tinctures. This also works best when all the liquids are a bit cooler than room temperature.

You may even find that you prefer your own creation to anything you could buy. In that case, you've just produced a spiced rum and you're only a venture capitalist away from becoming a Captain Morgan or a Sailor Jerry.

Cordials

You have now, by tiny experiential probings, just crossed to the boundary between playful student and cordial impresario. Let's leap over.

Cordials are generally agreed to be sweet mixtures of herb in alcohol. They were originally sold as medicinal compounds, often compounded by monks. The archetype is Chartreuse.

Take the best of your confections and recreate it using twice as much flavor as you used in your first attempt. Make a tincture that smells strongly of something other than mere alcohol. Then add some sugar. Try a tablespoon (15 g) in a 2 ounce (50 ml) portion of rum. Let the tincture age for two weeks, then chill the mixture thoroughly and taste when it's cold.

What do you have there? An after-dinner drink? A blast of bitters to cure your mouth of dailiness so you can begin a pleasant evening? Or perhaps an ingredient for a cocktail?

Now think backwards. Strawberries are about to come in season. Perhaps you should make a white rum and black pepper cordial. I wonder what would happen if you cut and crushed some beautifully fresh and ripe strawberries, doused them with your rum and pepper (rumper?) mix and sprinkled a bit of sugar on top. (Of course, you will have strained the grains of crushed pepper out before serving.) Actually, I don't wonder, I know— it's a knockout.

You could take this even further and soak the berries for a day or a week and use the fruit and cordial as a topping for ice cream or pound cake.

What other fresh fruits are just waiting for a custom designed cordial treatment? Mango with rosemary rum? Bananas with rum caramel? Will you take some of your fruit and rum and go back to the beginning and make a cocktail?

Imagine a giant keyboard and imagine yourself sitting, thirsty and curious before it. Any flavor that's soluble in alcohol or water (and that's most of them) could be one of your keys. The flavors are grouped: spices, fruits, wood and cane, flowers and herbs. How exciting. How thoroughly modern. Let's play!

Rum Tasting Kit contains the following items:
1) A selection of nine or more empty spice bottles.
2) A box to hold them in (The Rumelier used an old Goslings box).
3) A bottle of white rum (The Rumelier used Mount Gay).
4) Oak chips.
5) Molasses.
6) Vanilla Beans.
7) Cinnamon Sticks.
8) Pickling Spice.
9) Various Dried Fruits.
10) Nutmeg.
11) A bottle of fine aged rum.

About the Author

Lynn Hoffman is a man with no evident sense of direction. He has been a merchant seaman, anthropology professor, photographer, culinary arts teacher, chef, and cab driver. He's published three novels, *The Bachelor's Cat, Philadelphia Personal*, and *bang BANG*. He's also written *The New Short Course in Wine* and the *Short Course in Beer* and published over one hundred and fifty poems in literary journals. *Radiation Days*, his memoir of a funny year with cancer was published in July 2014 and these days, he wanders around doing a one-man show based on the experience and leading wine and beer tastings for charitable and educational groups. Most of the time he just loafs and fishes.

His romance with rum began when he lived in St.Croix in the 1970s. He has always thought that rum has the potential to be a profoundly beautiful drink, certainly the equal of bourbon and even approaching Cognac.

His poem, "The Would-be Lepidopterist," has been nominated for a Pushcart Prize. Other poetry has appeared in *Angelic Dynamo*, *Melusine*, *gutter eloquence*, *Off the Coast*, *Waterways*, *Abramelin*, *Referential*, *The Broad Street Review*, *Sephyrus*, and *Short, Fast, and Deadly*.

Born in Brooklyn and now a happy resident of Philadelphia, he teaches culinary arts and beverage management courses in Drexel University's Culinary Program. He has a daughter, Spencer Maeve Hoffman, who is a practicing attorney in New York City.

Short Course in Beer

An Introduction to Tasting and Talking about the World's Most Civilized Beverage

by Lynn Hoffman

"A tuition-free ride from beginner to beer aficionado. Students learn how beer's made; how to properly pour, pair, and taste it; and even better, how to talk about it. A dictionary of beer jargon and a beer-style guide—which both take a friendly, nonacademic tone—prove indispensable to the wannabe beer geek just getting his mug wet." —*Draft Magazine*

"Approaches the subject with an academic thoroughness, from the technical to the cultural, without ever getting too dry. It may be a pint-sized primer, but it's also thirst-quenchingly smart." —*Philadelphia Inquirer*

Straightforward and opinionated, *Short Course in Beer* is designed to turn the novice beer lover into an expert imbiber and the casual drinker into an enthusiast. Readers will come to understand the beauty of beer and the sources of its flavor, as well as learn which beers are worth our time and which are not. It's sure to stimulate lively conversations, presumably over a glass of equally lively beer.

$12.95 Paperback • ISBN 978-1-62914-495-5

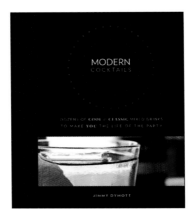

Modern Cocktails

Dozens of Cool and Classic Mixed Drinks to Make You the Life of the Party

by Jimmy Dymott

Dying to know how the pros mix drinks that look amazing and taste even better? Jimmy Dymott has been in the industry since the emergence of the modern cocktail bar, and he knows that hard work and the best ingredients are the true secrets to success behind the bar.

Jimmy Dymott shares sixty of his favorite and most impressive cocktails, from classics like the Old Fashioned and the Gin Fizz, to modern favorites like the Juicy Fruit. He includes recipes for drinks invented at his own bars—with mint, passion fruit, and fresh ingredients, they're always in high demand. Dymott explores the history of each drink—some spanning from eighth-century Persia to the American South in the 1800s. Plus, he offers the tools needed to make each drink pro, the types of bars out there to emulate, and great stories from Dymott's fifteen years in the cocktail scene. *Modern Cocktails* is the insider's introduction to the ingredients, the recipes, and the culture behind the top bars in the industry.

$17.95 Hardcover • ISBN 978-1-62873-642-7

Classic Cocktails

Time-Honored Recipes for the Home Bartender

by Amanda Hallay

Illustrated by David Wolfe

Classy ladies and dapper gents have their favorite vintage cocktail go-to, and now you can as well! From manhattans to pink ladies, gin fizzes to whiskey sours, Gibsons to stingers—and sixty additional cocktails—*Classic Cocktails* returns drinkers back to an age of sophisticated mixed drinks for the suave imbiber. While mixing your favorite cocktail, brush up on your pop culture trivia with quirky facts and snarky anecdotes. Recipes include:

- Bloody Mary
- Blue Hawaii
- Eggnog
- Gin sling
- Mai tai
- Mojito
- Old-fashioned
- Screwdriver
- Tequila sunrise
- Tom Collins
- White Russian
- And many more!

Also included is information on serving suggestions, glassware, and remedies for curing the occasional hangover. So harness your inner mixologist, break out the jar of maraschino cherries, and transport yourself and your friends to a time when "classic" cocktails were the only mixed drinks out there.

$14.95 Paperback • ISBN 978-1-62914-529-7

100 Classic Cocktails

The Ultimate Guide to Crafting Your Favorite Cocktails

by Sean Moore

This enjoyable collection includes all of your favorite cocktails, from recipes invented fairly recently—like the cosmopolitan, which only dates to the late eighties—to recipes dating all the way to the nineteenth century—the Tom Collins was first recorded in writing in 1876 by Jerry Thomas in his *Bon Vivant's Companion*. Readers will discover recipes on a variety of well-known cocktails, including:

- Brandy Alexander
- Metropolitan
- Aperol spritz
- Mimosa
- Bramble
- Gibson
- Pink lady
- Amaretto sour
- Dark and stormy
- Tequila sunrise
- Jungle juice
- Lemon drop
- Old fashioned
- And many more

Each easy-to-follow recipe is paired with beautiful, full-color photographs. Impress friends with your new classic cocktail expertise, or enjoy a relaxing night in with your favorite cocktail.

$19.95 Hardcover • ISBN 978-1-62914-703-1

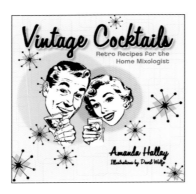

Vintage Cocktails

Retro Recipes for the Home Mixologist

by Amanda Hallay

Illustrations by David Wolfe

Anything you can mix and pour into a glass is now termed a "cocktail," but those drinks usually pale in comparison with the truly classic cocktails. *Vintage Cocktails* returns drinkers to an age of manhattans, pink ladies, gin fizzes, and whiskey sours. Included with the recipes are quirky cultural facts as well as serving suggestions, what to have stocked in your bar at all times, and how to cure the occasional hangover.

$16.95 Hardcover • ISBN 978-1-61608-394-6

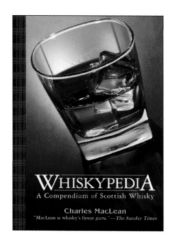

Whiskypedia

A Compendium of Scottish Whisky

by Charles MacLean

The flavor of Scotch whisky is as much influenced by history, craft, and tradition as it is by science. Individual distilleries give their whiskies unique characteristics. These characteristics do not arise magically (as was once thought), nor are they solely the result of the region (as is still thought, by some). They have their roots in the craft and custom of the distillery and of the district in which it is located, but the key influences upon flavor are the distilling equipment itself, how it is operated, and how the spirit is matured.

Whiskypedia explores these influences. For the first time, the flavor and character of every malt whisky distilled in Scotland is explored with reference to how it is made. Introductory sections provide an historical overview, an examination of regional differences, and an explanation of the contribution made by each stage of the production process. This compendium is a comprehensive guide to all the distilleries in Scotland (both malt and grain). Each entry provides a brief account of the distillery's history and curiosities, lists the bottlings which are currently available, details how the whisky is made, and explores the flavor and character of each make. Malt whisky is the quintessential "spirit of place," and this element of the story has been captured by John MacPherson's camera in specially commissioned images that complement the text.

$14.95 Paperback • ISBN 978-1-62087-107-2

The Joy of Home Distilling

The Ultimate Guide to Making Your Own Vodka, Whiskey, Rum, Brandy, Moonshine, and More

by Rick Morris

The Joy of Home Distilling is a complete guide for beginner and intermediate distillers. Readers will learn about every facet of distilling, from yeast styles and nutritional requirements to the different methods of distillation and equipment, and postdistillation processes. Author Rick Morris, who has been selling distillation equipment for years, even includes his own recipes for different types of spirits and drink recipes.

By learning not just how to distill, but also what is happening at each step and why it is necessary, readers will be armed with the information they need to experiment with their own spirits and concoct their own recipes.

Topics covered include:
- Keeping safety first when working with flammable materials, such as ethanol
- What distillation is and common misconceptions about the process
- The legalities surrounding distilling alcohol at home
- What yeast is, what it does, and how to ensure you get a strong, complete fermentation
- Step-by-step instructions for the different processes, from bucket to bottle
- The difference between spirit types and how to produce each
- Carbon filtering—when it's necessary, when to filter, and why you filter
- Flavoring and aging your spirits

$14.95 Paperback • ISBN 978-1-62914-586-0

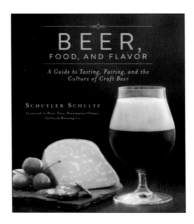

Beer, Food, and Flavor

A Guide to Tasting, Pairing, and the Culture of Craft Beer

by Schuyler Schultz

Foreword by Peter Zien

"From lessons in cheese-and-brew pairings to sketching a menu for a multi-course, beer-pairing dinner party . . . [this] excellent, 300-page guide to beer and food is a steal." —Evan S. Benn, Esquire.com

"An engaging look at American craft beer through the eyes of a working chef. If you want to know how to bring craft beer into your culinary life, this book will take you all the way there." —Garrett Oliver, brewmaster of The Brooklyn Brewery, author of *The Brewmaster's Table*, and editor in chief of *The Oxford Companion to Beer*

"Yes, great beer can change your life," writes chef Schuyler Schultz in *Beer, Food, and Flavor*. Here is your authoritative guide to exploring the diverse array of flavors found in craft beer—and the joys of pairing those flavors with great food to transform everyday meals into culinary events. Armed with the precise tasting techniques and pairing strategies offered inside, readers will find that participating in the growing craft beer community is now easier than ever. *Beer, Food, and Flavor* will enable you to learn about the top craft breweries in your region, seek out new beer styles and specialty brews with confidence, create innovative menus, and pair craft beer with fine food, whether at home or while dining out.

$19.95 Hardcover • ISBN 978-1-61608-679-4

Brewing Porters and Stouts

Origins, History, and 60 Recipes for Brewing Them at Home Today

by Terry Foster

From the enduring global dominance of Guinness to exciting new craft porters to the resurgence of Russian imperial stouts, porters and stouts are among the most popular beer styles today among homebrewers and craft beer drinkers alike. In *Brewing Porters and Stouts,* widely respected beer and brewing writer Terry Foster presents the history and development of these styles as well as the guidance and expertise necessary to successfully homebrew them yourself.

The book opens with the history of the styles, including the invention of porter in eighteenth-century England and how stouts were born from porters (stouts were originally bolder and stronger—or *stout*—porters). It details their development in the United Kingdom, and introduction to Ireland and eventually the United States, where they remained popular even as they fell out of favor in Britain and then surged in popularity as the craft brewing revolution took hold. Foster then goes on to explore the many substyles of porters and stouts, providing commercial examples and showcasing some of the most exciting developments in craft brewing today, before breaking down the ingredients, including the various malts as well as special flavorings—such as vanilla, coffee, chocolate, and even bourbon—and finally the yeasts, hops, and waters that are well suited to brewing these styles. Finally, Foster provides a collection of sixty recipes—up to six for each substyle—showcasing the variety and range of ingredients explored in the book and providing both extract and all-grain instructions.

$16.95 Paperback • ISBN 978-1-62914-511-2

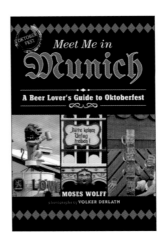

Meet Me in Munich

A Beer Lover's Guide to Oktoberfest

by Moses Wolff

Munich's Oktoberfest, held each year since 1810 from late September through the first weekend in October, is one of the most famous events in Germany. It is a beer drinker's paradise—over the course of sixteen days, more than six million visitors consume nearly two million gallons of specially brewed Oktoberfest beer. For the first-time visitor to the Wiesn (a meadow near Munich's center dedicated to the festival), Oktoberfest can be a little overwhelming. Fortunately, Moses Wolff hasn't missed a day of Oktoberfest in years, and he knows the festival like the back of his hand.

$19.95 Hardcover • ISBN 978-1-62636-258-1

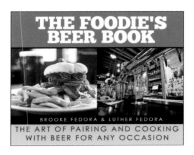

The Foodie's Beer Book
The Art of Pairing and Cooking with Beer for Any Occasion
by Brooke Fedora and Luther Fedora

The Foodie's Beer Book is the ultimate celebration of beer and food pairings. A glass of beer alone can be a splendid thing, but when incorporated into your cooking and served alongside the dish, it can be a symphony of flavor. Chefs Brooke and Luther Fedora explain the many ways beer can enrich and enhance a dish or an entire meal by providing a wealth of recipes and suggested pairings.

Begin by exploring beer varieties and their characteristics, helping you to learn the various flavor notes that are the foundation for cooking and pairings. A hoppy beer, for example, can add bite to a dish and is best for batters and light dishes, but is inappropriate for long simmering dishes where it instead strengthens the inherent bitterness of the dish. Malt, on the other hand, can add a mellow sweetness that is pleasing in stewed dishes and marinades. Have fun with dinner again, as you explore the wide variety of flavor profiles made possible through the addition of beer—from a traditional cassoulet laced with a malty dark ale to the lemony snap of a light Berliner Weisse paired with a lemon sorbet.

Recipes are broken down by various regions and seasons, making it possible to drink your way through the calendar year with recipes and tips for various events and holidays, including Saint Patrick's Day, New Year's Eve, Mardi Gras, Christmas, and Oktoberfest. So grab yourself a pint and dig in!

$24.95 Hardcover • ISBN 978-1-62873-682-3

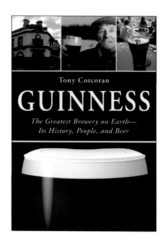

Guinness

The Greatest Brewery on Earth—Its History, People, and Beer

by Tony Corcoran

There is no other company, industry, or premises more closely aligned with its hometown than Guinness's St. James's Gate Brewery and the city of Dublin. From the company's modest beginnings in 1759 to its heyday in the late nineteenth and early twentieth centuries and its continued strength into the twenty-first century, Guinness has had an enormous influence over the city's economic, social, and cultural life.

In this warm and fascinating piece of history, Tony Corcoran examines the magnitude of the brewery's operation, and the working lives of the thousands of Dubliners who have depended on Guinness for their livelihood. The company's unusually progressive treatment of its workers—health care, training, and housing—is revealed in detail, as is the Guinness family's philanthropy and compassion toward the less well-off residents of the city. Corcoran also explores the important roles of the strong-willed women in each generation of the Guinness dynasty. *Guinness* is full of anecdotes, humor, and historical insights into one of Dublin's most important and best-loved institutions.

"Whenever I bleed, I am always surprised to see that my blood is not black. Certainly, when you consider that I was born into two Guinness families, had two Guinness grandfathers and five Guinness uncles, and was on the premises of Guinness before I could walk, I am as much a product of Guinness as the black stuff itself." —Tony Corcoran

$14.95 Paperback • ISBN 978-1-62636-076-1

A Scent of Champagne

8,000 Champagnes Tested and Rated

by Richard Juhlin

A Scent of Champagne is a luxury volume on the world's most elegant beverage—by world renowned champagne expert Richard Juhlin, with an introduction by Édouard Cointreau.

In this beautiful and heavily illustrated volume, the world's foremost champagne expert, Richard Juhlin, takes the reader on a journey to the geographical area of Champagne and through the history of the beverage. With rich photography to accompany the text, he explains how to arrange tastings, how to develop one's sense of smell, and why the setting where you drink champagne is important. He also includes personal anecdotes about his lifelong journey from teacher to connoisseur as well as a reference guide describing and ranking an incredible eight thousand champagne houses, types, and vintages.

Sit back and enjoy Juhlin's graceful prose with a lovely glass of champagne, the beverage that has come to epitomize luxury and elegance. This is a must-have edition for any serious collector and lover of champagne.

$75.00 Hardcover • ISBN 978-1-62636-072-3